CW00673550

Green Harts

The Story of Two Lifelong Friends

Paul Hart and Norman Foweraker

Copyright © 2024 Paul Hart and Norman Foweraker

ISBN: 9781917425650

All rights reserved, including the right to reproduce this book, or portions thereof in any form. No part of this text may be reproduced, transmitted, downloaded, decompiled, reverse engineered, or stored, in any form or introduced into any information storage and retrieval system, in any form or by any means, whether electronic or mechanical without the express written permission of the author.

Dedication

Dedicated to the late Edna May Leaman (formerly Hart).

A wonderful, hardworking mum for her sons, Paul, Philip and the late Patrick as well as stepson Peter; and also, a second mum to Norman.

A shining example of a caring member of the human race who kept us all on the right path.

Thank you, Mum, affectionately known to Norman as 'Aunty Ed'.

Foreword

by Billy Rafferty – Former Player Plymouth Argyle

This book was first contemplated when two men were having lunch at a Plymouth Argyle football match away at Forest Green Rovers on 16 November 2019.

Paul Hart and his lifelong friend, Norman Foweraker, whilst sat at a table surrounded by fellow Argyle fans, began reminiscing about their experiences from school days in the 1960s to the present day. The main thread which underpinned their adventures through life was a joint love of their football team, known affectionately to many football fans as 'Argyle'.

Norman's wife, Deb, saw that the duo had a captive audience around the table that day and suggested the two friends should share both their football and life experiences with a wider audience. The two realised their story was more than just about friendship, football and growing up; it was a story also of social history and past times. So it was that they decided to write and publish this book. They hope that it evokes memories and, for all, a smile.

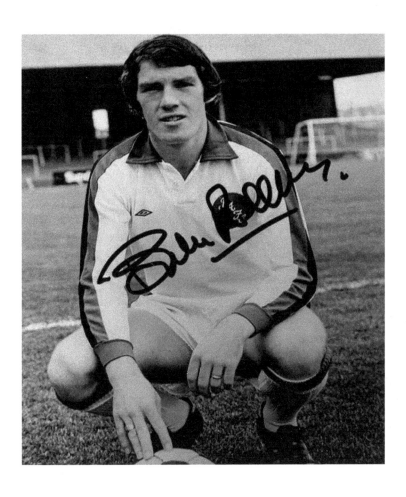

Acknowledgements:

Our heartfelt thanks to Debbie (Deb) Foweraker for her support, enthusiasm and drive.

To Paul's brother Philip for his advice and contribution.

To Matt Ellacott Photography.

Thanks also to John Hore and Billy Rafferty.

August 1974

Paul (left), Deb and Norman (right)

at St James's Park, London

CHAPTER

First Game

Wednesday 31 August 1960
Plymouth Argyle v Sheffield United
Division Two – 7.30 pm Kick Off
Paul:
I will always remember this game as a nine-year-old as it was the first time I went to Plymouth Argyle. I was already a football mad kid, and when my Uncle Kenny offered to take me to the game, I thought Christmas had come early.

Kenny was a big Argyle fan and normally drove one of the many football special buses that used to line up outside the Devonport end Stand on a Saturday. The Devonport end of the ground was, and still is to this day, where the main 'choir' congregates and instigates songs and chants in support of Argyle. The opposite end of the ground which housed, and indeed still houses, a mixture of home supporters and away fans is known as the Barn Park end, whilst the two remaining stands are known as the Lyndhurst and Mayflower Stands.

That night we made our way to the game and stood on the Mayflower side. I remember being lifted down to the front where I was right up against the railings.

Everything appeared so big. The grandstand, floodlights and the pitch seemed huge; in fact, the whole place felt massive. I remember so well the thrill of being in such an electric atmosphere and when the players entered the field, I could barely contain my excitement. I will never forget the smell of the liniment as the teams came onto the pitch. Argyle won the game 2–0 with goals from George Kirby and Billy Wright. I was hooked.

My first game under the lights, a crowd of over 24,000, that smell of liniment, and Argyle won. Little did I know what a journey I was to embark on as a Plymouth Argyle fan.

Norman:

Unfortunately, I am not able to remember the first game I watched at Home Park; the home ground of Plymouth Argyle Football Club, but then I am older than Paul, and whilst we may have started our supporting of Argyle at slightly different times, I do remember the buses queuing outside of the Devonport end. Incidentally, my Uncle Frank was also a bus driver and later went on to become an inspector with Plymouth City Transport.

I also remember seeing such Argyle heroes as Harry Penk, Gordon Fincham and Wilf Carter to name but a few. George Robertson also played and I well remember much later, whilst in my local amateur football days, I played against George who was many years my senior but was still able to make me look as if I should have been playing kindergarten football.

One thing I am certain of is that my journey as a supporter of the Greens, like Paul's, also began at a very young age and, in many ways, Argyle became a very important part of my early years and my passion for the Pilgrims is ever present.

Plymouth Argyle are nicknamed the 'Pilgrims' due to the Plymouth connection with the Pilgrim Fathers who set sail from Plymouth, Devon, in the early seventeenth century, embarking upon their historic journey of discovery, eventually arriving in what is now known as Cape Cod, in the United States of America, where the colony of Plymouth was founded.

The colours of the football club have been predominately green and white throughout its history; hence they are referred to by their supporters as the 'Greens'.

Autographs – A Sign of the Times

Paul:

Having been totally smitten by my first game at Home Park in the August of 1960, it seemed logical to me that the next step was to collect players' autographs, not only those of Argyle players but of the opposition as well. Consequently, you will not be surprised, dear reader, that I was amongst hundreds of people queuing patiently at the old Plymouth Co-op department store on the morning of Saturday 8 October 1960.

The Co-op building was almost destroyed in 1941 during the Blitz of Plymouth but was rebuilt and reopened in 1953 as a department store selling a variety of goods and services. In 1958 it was renamed Co-operative House. The building closed as the Co-op in 2010.

The reason for this early morning excursion was that there were three famous Middlesborough FC footballers on a stage that had been erected temporarily on the ground floor of the Co-op. One of these footballers, little did I know then how famous he would become, was the great Brian Clough. In those days my dear mother would not let me go into town alone, due to the fact that I was only nine years old, and so she was with me on this particular day as we moved gradually closer to the stage. It seemed like an eternity before we got there, and I was so excited to get my first three autographs. I asked Mr Clough for two autographs; even back then he would only sign one autograph per person. 'Why would you want two, young man?' he asked; too scared to answer, I sheepishly left the stage. Later that afternoon, Clough was amongst the goal scorers in an exciting 3–3 draw at Home Park.

In the Argyle side that day was a certain Johnny Newman, whom I now speak to on the morning of every cup final day. I came to know Johnny through a 'friend of a friend' who lives in Derby and is great friends with him.

3

The three of them have a ritual where they meet in Derby on every cup final day. On one such day a few years ago, I received a surprise telephone call from my friend who said, 'You will never guess who is with me and wishes to speak to you because of your involvement with the Plymouth Argyle ex-players association.' (Of which there is more later in this book.) It was Johnny Newman and because it was cup final day when I spoke to him, it has become a tradition that Johnny and I speak on every cup final day. Johnny played for Argyle from 1960 until 1967.

I was completely absorbed in autograph collecting. Every school holiday was spent at Home Park collecting signatures. It was not uncommon, in order to collect these signatures, for lads to buy large blue A5 covered books from Underhill's, a stationery shop just down from the library which was then located in Tavistock Road, Plymouth, but has since been relocated a short distance away to Taylor Maxwell House, Armada Way. I was one of those lads. Back then all the players used to wear suits to training, and we would wait outside the players' entrance until they finished their session. I remember goalkeeper Dave MacLaren used to make everyone line up in single file before he would sign. If you stepped out of line, he would cease signing until order was restored. The other players were happy for us to swarm around them like bees until we were close enough to thrust our books into their hands.

Friday nights before a home game soon became a ritual. I was now allowed into town with friends, and we often descended on the city centre hotels. Most visiting teams used to stay at the Grand Hotel or the Astor Hotel on Plymouth Hoe.

I was one of about twenty regulars from across the city who would arrive at the hotel for 5.30 pm. Teams then used to go to the cinema and, as films were double features, if we didn't get them before they went in, we would return to the hotel on the Saturday morning.

On Saturday mornings it was not unusual for the Grand Hotel to have a wedding, and it's fair to say they were not amused to have us kids hanging around on the staircase. It was a battle of wits between us and the concierge, who constantly told us to remain at the bottom of the stairs. He was fighting a losing battle as one by one we crept to the top of the stairs, hoping to stop a player walking by. The blue book was starting to fill up.

The first time I ran onto the pitch was to try and get an autograph. It was 11 November 1964 and we had just beaten Stoke City 3–1 in the Fourth Round of the League Cup, with Frank Lord scoring a hat-trick. I remember running on from the lower Mayflower thrusting my blue book at the first Stoke player in sight; his name was Alan Philpott.

I continued collecting autographs until the early 70s and built up a superb collection, after which I discovered better ways to spend my Friday nights (girls). I was married in the summer of 1978 and my autograph days were over, or so I thought.

Fast forward to 1990; I was working for the House of Fraser and now had a ten-year-old daughter. I had been working away from home since 1986, coming back to Plymouth most weekends or on a Tuesday night if Argyle were at home.

Sadly, Rachel (my daughter) was diagnosed with acute Lymphoblastic Leukaemia in the spring of 1991, resulting in me missing almost all of the 1992/3 season. Still working away from home and with Rachel in and out of hospital, even I didn't have the bottle to go to football on a Saturday afternoon although I was tempted on more than one occasion. My dear mother also passed away in 1993; it was certainly a year to forget.

I was back with a vengeance for the 93/94 season and guess what – Rachel and I both had season tickets and we enjoyed our football from the Lyndhurst side. It was a great season with Argyle losing to Burnley in the play-offs.

Whilst being involved in the writing of this book, I have learned that Rachel's reason for going to Argyle was to spend quality time with me; I was still working away. It wasn't until the summer of 2023 that Rachel informed me why she had wanted us to attend Argyle matches together. I know now that even though she has confessed to her extreme dislike of football, she wanted to come in order to spend time with me. I had no idea and it made me feel so humble.

We continued to watch from the Lyndhurst the following season, with one big difference. We started hanging around the players' entrance after the game. Then the inevitable happened! Rachel asked me to get the autographs of some of the Argyle players for her; that's my story, anyway. Although Rachel may say it was me that wanted them really.

That was it – my addiction resurfaced and I continued to collect signatures of Argyle and opposition players until 2008. However, to this very day I still collect one signature (I hope the late, great Mr Clough would have been impressed) of every Argyle player to adorn the green and white shirt. It was during this second period of autograph collecting that I met Andy Riddle and Tom Finnie and when gradually my introduction and involvement with the Argyle Legends began.

Saturday 27 January 1962
Plymouth Argyle v Tottenham Hotspur
FA Cup – Fourth Round
Paul:

I was now ten and a half years old and had been allowed to go to Argyle with my mates since I was ten. I lived in Penlee Place, Mutley. Plymouth was great in the 60s and most of the local kids in the area went to Hyde Park Junior School and were football mad.

We spent hours playing football on Lisson Grove bomb site (there were numerous bomb sites around the city after the Blitz of the Second World War) re-enacting games involving the big clubs of the day and so when we drew Tottenham (also known as Spurs) in the cup, we were ecstatic. Spurs were the best team in the country at the time with their pass-and-move football and had great players throughout their team. However, since Argyle had beaten another first division side, West Ham United, in the third round, we all believed we could win.

We had a routine, even in those days. Some of the boys played for Hyde Park Junior School on a Saturday morning and so we would leave home at about half past nine in the morning and be gone all day; the route was always the same: up Belgrave Road, across the main road on Mutley Plain, down Ford Park Road, turn right into Trelawney Road and down to Barn Park. That's where Hyde Park played their home games, always with a 10.30 am kick off. We had never been watched by so many people, such were the numbers arriving early in order to gain a place on the terraces at Home Park.

In those days we used to watch the games from the Barn Park end, which seemed to be where young kids started before graduating to the Devonport end. I can't remember what time the gates opened but we were in the ground really early. I think we paid half a crown (30p) for our ticket. The souvenir A4-sized programme was a shilling (5p). There was no segregation and the Barn Park end was full of good-humoured Tottenham fans. I remember us giving several of them a bit of lip before running off.

It was all good fun until I fell over and cut my knee. It was a deep cut and I was taken to the St John's Ambulance hut for repairs. I remember the first aid guy saying it was a nasty cut and I would have to go home and miss the game. Thank goodness he was only joking! Although I think me bursting into tears may have helped my cause. I hobbled off, knee bandaged, and went to the front of the Barn Park end, right behind the goal.

The game was brilliant, and Argyle played really well. A 5–1 defeat would suggest otherwise, but it seemed every time Tottenham shot, they scored and they were 3–0 up at half time, all the goals scored at the Barn Park end. It was a tremendous occasion, easily the biggest crowd I'd been in, over 40,000. Half time came and went; one of the records played was 'The Young Ones' by Cliff Richard and the Shadows, who were number one in the charts at the time.

The second half was like the first; Argyle played well, but Tottenham's finishing was brilliant. With Spurs leading 4–0 came the moment we had been waiting for: the late great Peter Anderson scored right in front of us at the Barn Park end. The crowd erupted; you'd have thought we had won the cup. Not to be denied, Tottenham scored a fifth from, I think, Jimmy Greaves.

It took ages to get out of the ground, an eternity to get to the 'Ten Steps Start Here' sign (put in place to warn supporters of the downward journey to the exit) behind the Barn Park end. In fact, it took so long I went to Stephen's Bakery at the end of Mutley Plain to make sure I secured my copy of the *Football Herald*; then it was off home to read all about the incredible match and tell my mother and younger brother all about it.

An amazing day and I knew then it was 'Argyle till I die'.

Norman:

Like Paul and his mates, we lads from Wordsworth Road would have some cracking games of football, no doubt taking on the roles of our soccer heroes, but our games were usually in the street. There was a goal at one end of the pitch, which consisted of a drain cover on one side of the road and a lamp post on the other (the lamp post made a great floodlight), whilst the other goal was made up of two drain covers; fortunately, traffic in those days was generally fairly light. Obviously, there were some interruptions when the occasional vehicle 'happened' upon our pristine tarmac pitch.

I remember on one occasion a car came down the road, thereby interrupting what was almost certainly one of the best footballing moves I am sure to have been undertaken during this high intensity game and, true to the frustrations often felt by many of the great stars of the game, I possibly overreacted somewhat and threw a piece of rubble from the road in the direction of the vehicle. Unfortunately for me, the driver took exception to this, got out of his vehicle and approached my mother, who perchance was sweeping the path at the front of our house. He, shall we say, expressed his severe dissatisfaction at what I considered to be my perfectly justified reaction. Sadly, for me, my mother was armed with a long-handled sweeping brush and agreed with his version of events; justice was swift and severely administered. As a result, the thought of ever undertaking the role of 'sweeper' in our street games was not in the forefront of my mind.

Paul, who I did not know at the time of the Tottenham game, may have cut his knee, but I think he must have wanted subconsciously to emulate me, since I still carry a scar on my right knee from where I came to grief on the

Wordsworth Stadium football pitch, AKA Wordsworth Road.

I recall on the day of the Spurs game, as an eleven-year-old, arriving at Home Park full of excitement and anticipation at seeing my team take on the might of Spurs. I think I got into the Devonport end at about noon and, at that time, at the front there was loads of room for me to consume my Ivor Dewdney pasty (Ivor Dewdney pasties have been a well-known local brand for many years) but, by the time kick off came, there wasn't much room for arm movement in the crowd of 40,040. Perhaps it was just as well because, as Paul has stated, we went on to lose 5–1. Only two of the goals were scored at the Devonport end and both of them were for Spurs. Little did I know at that time that my best chum and Argyle compatriot-to-be was nestling somewhere amongst the huge crowd in the opposite end of the ground.

So here we have it, two different views at Home Park, one from the Barn Park end and one from the Devonport end. Two young boys who at that time were completely unaware of the lifelong friendship that was destined to develop and that Plymouth Argyle would play such a pivotal role in their respective lives.

The Year 1962 – Memories Continued

Saturday 28 April 1962
Plymouth Argyle v Liverpool
Division Two – 3.15 pm Kick Off
Norman:

I remember being in the crowd at Home Park when the mighty Liverpool, then believe it or not a Division Two side, played Argyle. Liverpool had already won promotion to Division One, the top tier, and Argyle players provided a guard of honour when Liverpool entered the field of play, only for the reds to be heckled at the end of the game, having won 3–2, for their use of what many Argyle fans on the day would have considered dubious tactics.

The goalkeeper in the Liverpool team was one Jim Furnell, who would later go on to play 183 times for Argyle and who, for many supporters, was possibly Argyle's best goalkeeper of all time. Incidentally, the Greens finished fifth in Division Two that season.

The Meeting of 'Harty' and 'Storm' – September 1962

Paul Hart, known fondly as 'Harty', grew up at Penlee Place, Mutley, Plymouth with two younger brothers, Philip and Patrick. Very sadly, Paul's father passed away when Paul was six years old and on the sad day when his father was laid to rest, Paul's mother, Edna, was informed that Patrick had been formally diagnosed as both mentally and physically disabled.

Norman Foweraker, in later years to be known as 'Storm' (this nickname was given to him by his work colleagues after a famous American general, Herbert Norman Schwarzkopf Junior, who had two nicknames, one of which was 'Stormin Norman'), grew up in Wordsworth Road, which he always referred to as being located in Higher Camels Head but, in reality, the area was known as Swilly, which many considered to be a notorious area of Plymouth, often visited by the local police, the irony of which will be revealed later. Norman was one of six children, his siblings being Freddie, Maureen, Michael, Keith and Christine.

So, as previously mentioned, Paul attended Hyde Park Infants and Junior School, Norman went to Camels Head Infants and Junior School, both boys amazingly passed the eleven-plus and at that time neither was really aware of the academic door they had potentially opened. The duo first encountered one another in September 1962 when they were placed in the same year group at Sutton High School, and so the story begins...

The Swilly Boy

Norman:

In those days, growing up in Swilly was probably seen by many as challenging, to say the least, and whilst I accept there were difficult times, there was also a sense of community amongst the majority of folks who lived in the area, most of whom just wanted to live their lives in harmony and look out for one another.

I developed some good friendships and will never forget my roots; after all, we are what we are and as the saying goes: 'You can take the boy out of Plymouth but you can't take Plymouth out of the boy.'

Yes, there was a faction in the area who for whatever reason were always on the 'wrong side of the fence' and sadly that minority, as is probably the same in most cities, was the main reason for the adverse reputation of the area and, without becoming too philosophical, it is my view that I, along with so many, was brought up to show respect to others and to treat them as I would expect to be treated myself.

I would like to think that ideology has stood me in good stead in my many dealings with others over the years. My parents didn't have a lot, as was the case with many on our estate, and when one talks of deprivation, I will agree that from an economic perspective that may have been the case.

I can remember we had a coal fire in our council house front room (most of us probably call it a lounge today) but coal was expensive and when the fire was extinguished, the ashes would be placed in a heap in the garden. My dear dad could often be found 'kicking over the traces', looking for pieces of coal that had not fully burned so they could be reused. I can also recall when I was a little older, my parents had separated and I was living in the Devonport area of Plymouth with my mother, sister Christine, and eventually an Amazon green parrot (see, even our pet was of the Argyle persuasion) whom we named Polly. I have a vivid memory of wearing shoes that had holes in the soles and enterprisingly I had cardboard in them to somewhat unsuccessfully protect my feet from the elements, but again such experiences I feel only go to make you stronger and more resolute. As I have already said, I will never forget my roots for I believe they helped me determine my future path in life.

When I retired from my chosen career (which I will refer to later in this book), I eventually took a job working in a school in Exeter with young people who had behavioural issues and I am certain that my experiences growing up helped me to empathise with and understand their frustrations even though some of them may have been fans of a certain team from 'up the road'.

I probably learned more about life in my early years living in Swilly than perhaps I realise; yes, it was tough at times and, like so many, I was on a carousel where some felt they were born into a certain genre and went around on that carousel, being insulated within that world. You then maybe married and had children, who continued on the same carousel, but we are all our own people; we have our own brains and can make our own decisions. I passed the eleven-plus exam and moved to Sutton High School; I was considered, I'm sure, an exception. People from our estate stayed on the carousel and went to the local secondary school; how many, I wonder, were not able to realise their full potential because they were forced to remain on that roundabout?

Was I lucky? Maybe, certainly in as much as I realised at a relatively young age that you can make your own decisions in life and, whilst I have many happy memories of my early years in Swilly in particular, I decided that staying on the carousel was not for me. I guess my biggest bit of luck was meeting Deb (now my wife) who has been my rock for so many years; mind you, I would say she too

14

was so lucky to meet such a committed Argyle fan who was able to quite quickly induct her into the fold of the Green Army.

There were many difficult and dark days but for me the main staple, particularly after meeting my chum Paul, was the Argyle and the spirit of community supporting them brought. To this day, as season ticket holders in the Lyndhurst, Deb and I, not forgetting our son David, have fostered friendships with like-minded Greens whom we would never have known if it weren't for the love of the Argyle.

School Days

Sutton High School for Boys was a grand limestone Victorian building located in Regent Street, Plymouth. The school opened in 1897 as the Mount Street Higher Grade School. In 1926 it became Sutton Secondary School, later to become Sutton High School for Boys. The building was closed in 1984 but Sutton remained until 1986, having moved location as a school.

During our time at Sutton, the headmaster was Mr H J Bristow, affectionately known to us as Henry though at times not quite so affectionately.

Paul and Norman quickly became friends; in fact, Norman recounts they were so friendly that on one occasion whilst Paul was standing innocently chatting to another pupil leaning against a wall outside a classroom, Paul was oblivious to the act of friendship that was about to unfold from his chum.

Norman, having seen that Paul was unaware of Norm's presence, decided to announce his arrival by running the length of the corridor and launching himself like a demented banshee, with his knee about two feet off the ground connecting with Paul's thigh muscle, sending him unceremoniously into a heap on the floor. Norman has since acknowledged that today at Home Park, this would have been an instant red card; nevertheless, at the time, he was proud of the accuracy of his action and Paul has just about forgiven him.

Privileged

Norman:

I guess the word privileged is one that is often used by football fans who have been fortunate enough to witness some of the great players in action.

But has there ever been a greater member of the football family than the late Stanley Matthews, who was knighted in 1965 and became Sir Stanley Matthews in recognition of his service to football?

Maybe I am a bit biased, for I was privileged to see the great man in action at Home Park when he played at the age of forty-eight against Argyle in a Division Two game for Stoke City in front of a crowd of about 22,000.

The game took place on 23 March 1963 and my memory of seeing the maestro in action was being with my brother Freddie in the Lyndhurst (standing in those days); what a wizard of football was Stanley Matthews. Imagine playing professional football at that level at the age of forty-eight.

Not only a privilege to see, but I would say an honour. Incidentally, Stoke won the game 1–0 and went on to be Division Two champions in that season.

If only I had Paul's penchant for autograph collection, I could have obtained the signature of Stanley Matthews, a master of his trade.

Cap in the Park

Lunchtimes at Sutton High School often involved a trip to nearby Beaumont Park, where serious games of football took place.

Clearly, goalposts were necessary and school caps were an ideal solution to this problem. On one particular day after a furious game of football, Paul was extremely exhausted and felt it was in his best interest to retire from the afternoon lesson sessions at school.

Paul states: 'I well remember this incident; in fact, I was desperate to get back to afternoon lessons but, would you believe it, my school cap was one of those being used as a goalpost and when our game finished, a wayward dog came hammering across the park and ran off with my precious headgear. I spent the rest of the afternoon chasing said dog! Knowing the value of the cap and the necessity of wearing it back to school, I faced a dilemma: To follow the dog and recover said headgear or risk the wrath of the teaching staff by turning up hatless? I chose the former of the two options. Everyone else, including Norman, returned to school but by the time I had retrieved my cap, I felt that I was far too exhausted and late to attend the afternoon school sessions.

I presumed that this tale of woe, allied to my dedication to my school uniform, would be a perfectly valid reason when, the following day, I needed to explain the absence of the previous afternoon. Surprisingly, I was not believed. I don't think I was handed out any punishment; rather I think they felt that as I was such a lost cause at this point, it was easier to give me a reprimand.

To this day, I still cannot understand why they did not believe such an innovative tale.

Nails in the Hall

Physics and Chemistry were probably not subjects that greatly endeared themselves to Norman, nor he suspects Paul, except if they could participate in the chemistry sessions where H_2S, commonly known as Hydrogen sulfide (who said they couldn't be chemists), was created in the lab, generating a rotten egg smell, which could cause nasal discomfort to many around the school. Ironically, in Physics, Norman is proud to say that he can still recite the majority of Archimedes' Principle.

Notwithstanding these joyous and unsurpassed moments in the Science lessons, the majority were to them both dull and unnecessary. Norman well remembers one time when their Science teacher was taking a lesson in a classroom which was on the same floor as the main hall. The hall was in effect the main hub for most whole school activities. There was a stage from where the school hierarchy could address us mere mortals during assemblies and such like. The main hall flooring comprised a topcoat of what can be described as floorboards (probably planks of wood to us boys). As well as classrooms, the headmaster's office was on the same floor.

Norman and Paul both knew that their Science teacher had a soft spot for them and on this particular day, when the boys were bored and perhaps less attentive than their teacher wanted, clearly not wishing to hand them a detention, he instead sent them to the hall to count the nails in the planks of wood they would find there.

Not a problem, you may think, but their teacher did not teach Science for nothing; there was clearly a method in his apparent madness, for if whilst doing their calculations in the hall the headmaster should happen to appear, there was big trouble ahead for them which may have included dust flying from the seats of their respective derrieres!

They quickly did a mathematical calculation and returned to the classroom with their solution, only to be told by their favourite teacher that he had checked earlier that day and they were wrong (oh, how they wished they had listened more to their maths teacher!) and so he sent them out again. Norman for one wished their school uniform consisted of khaki trousers; thankfully the headmaster did not appear and they both probably avoided a length of bamboo being applied to a rather tender area of their respective anatomies.

What a star was their science teacher.

Team Coach

It's not every school boy who can say that after a very important and challenging lunchtime football fixture in their own personal Home Park (AKA Beaumont Park which was situated not far from their school) they are then transported from such an idyllic setting to their alleged place of work, known as Sutton High School.

However, this was the case for Paul and Norman when after one of these difficult lunchtime fixtures, an older and possibly not that much wiser fellow Argyle supporter, one George Taylor, happened on the two weary footballers as they began their trudge back to their place of education.

As it happened, George was driving the team bus which, believe it or not, doubled as a milk float, and so it was that the two of them accepted the invitation of a lift back to school and climbed aboard the said milk float, perching precariously amongst the crates of gold-top and rattling bottles.

As the team coach drew up alongside the main entrance to the school, George, clearly having decided to test his emergency braking skills, slammed on the brakes and both Paul and Norman flew unceremoniously off the coach, literally hitting the ground running, only to disappear at speed into the school playground, where they successfully avoided detection by the authoritarian prefects whom they are sure would have seen it as some sort of coup if they had been able to bring the boys to book.

Thank you, George.

Match Days at Harty's

Norman:

I had by now become almost an integral part of the Hart household and was, I think, considered by some as the fourth brother of the family. Paul's wonderful mum had become known to me as Mrs H, but as time went on, she affectionally became 'Aunty Ed'.

Computer games and the like were unheard of in those days but for us youngsters, Subbuteo was the be-all and end-all. Harty's house in Penlee Place was on three floors, with the front room on ground level and a kitchen on basement level where Mrs H could often be found completing various chores, one of which was the production of her wonderful meat and potato pie.

Subbuteo was and still is a tabletop reproduction of a real-life football match involving tiny figures on small bases. The figures which resemble footballers are then 'flicked' by means of the player's finger around a felt football pitch (which is probably about three quarters the size of the average dining table surface), allowing the miniature footballers to connect with a small plastic football which is about one third of the size of a table tennis ball. There is a small plastic goal at either end of the felt 'pitch', the object of the game being to score as many goals as possible in order to win the match, in the same way as a real football match. The game was 'all the rage' amongst us football-mad youngsters since the object of the exercise was to win a competitive game by outscoring your opponent, and of course, it was an opportunity to compete as your favourite team of heroes.

As I have mentioned, Subbuteo was the go-to game for us lads and the front room was often turned into a miniature version of Wembley or even, I suspect on occasions, what we now know as the Theatre of Greens (AKA Home Park). There were numerous players and attendees to the Hart household for these festivals of football at tabletop level and, of course, all games were played in a fair and sporting manner, although some, particularly Philip (the middle brother), may disagree.

Paul and I, along with possibly half of the local boys, would be crammed into the Penlee Place Stadium with dear Patrick (Paul's youngest brother) being in the corner in the 'disabled stand'.

Paul versus Philip – Philip scored, or so he thought; Paul was clearly well versed in his own version of Subbuteo rules: 'No, no, that was offside,' he said. The crowd watched on in awe as the two siblings entered into furious discussion; Paul refused to accept the goal. His younger sibling, realised he was not going to win the argument and continued trying to convince Paul that the goal should stand. Paul would not budge and then Philip, in absolute exasperation, delivered a sledgehammer blow to the match ball and stormed off with Mrs H shouting up from the kitchen in the depths of the building, 'What's going on up there?' Patrick was heard to exclaim 'OOOOhhhhhhh.'

Philip later went on to become a local referee, but I am not sure to this day if he fully understands the Subbuteo offside rule, which was probably invented by Paul.

French Connection

The dynamic duo were very popular amongst their peers, particularly when it came to the gratifying and stimulating subject of French on a Monday after the lads had attended an Argyle game on the previous Saturday.

There is some significance to the above comments; the popularity of the two boys in the French lesson may have been conditional upon them engaging with their wonderful French teacher: wonderful, yes; he had to be, since part of his spare time activities focused on volunteering as a match commentator at Argyle for hospital radio. Why would he not be a marvellous person? (They recall he actually was a very nice man.)

He would come into their Monday morning French soiree full of good intention to focus on getting them to GCE 'O' Level (today's equivalent of a GCSE) standard in the language of their *amis* from across the English Channel. However, ultimately they think his real intention was to teach them enough of the language to enable them to order a beer or a cup of coffee should they in future years visit the country. Norman remembers that in later years, paying some attention within the French lessons helped in no small way when one of his daughters broke her arm whilst on a family holiday and he went with her to hospital where English was barely spoken; he was able to communicate sufficiently with the hospital staff during a difficult time.

Returning to the French lessons, the task which usually befell Harty and Norman was to engage that lovely teacher of French in a 'full-on' résumé of the Argyle game from the previous weekend, and boy, were they good at their assignment.

In he would come:

'Good game on Saturday, sir.'

'I'm not talking about the match; we have French to do.'

'What a great game Norman Piper had.'

'No, he didn't; he was awful.'

'But, sir, he is an England under-23 international.'

We had him hooked! And so it went on, the analysis of the game and, of course, the reduction in the duration of the French lesson.

Norman and Harty are unable to recall what may have been the record amount of time they managed the clever distraction for; however, suffice it to say, they feel that the rest of the French class of the day would have felt the two of them should have received some sort of medal for their expertise: '*Allez les Verts.*'

Henry

Henry Menyena was one of our best school chums. We do not make this statement lightly nor because Henry was prepared to challenge any pupil who brought into question his superiority as the toughest and most uncompromising member of our school year. Whilst it was undoubtedly true that being Henry's friend was at that time a matter of self-preservation, the two of us were a canny pair.

It was also a fact that Henry actually was, underneath that tough exterior, just a really nice guy who didn't suffer fools gladly and, as you may have realised by now, the two amigos were perhaps a little stupid, but they were certainly no fools. Paul recalls that, he was humbled, thankful and safe in the knowledge that being arguably the most diminutive member of the Henry clique, he always felt secure and indeed his good looks remain (in his opinion anyway) to this day.

Norman well remembers being lookout for Henry who would be in a cubicle in the boys' toilets, puffing on one of the cigarettes he had managed to purchase probably using his school bus fare. Henry has informed us that Norman would sub Henry for his bus fare; although Norman doesn't recall this, he does wonder how much interest he could have attracted by now on those donations! Having been Henry's lookout all those years ago has proven to be a positive experience for Norman as he considers he still possesses wonderful whistling skills to this day.

Both Norman and Paul have had the privilege of speaking with their old school chum, who now lives in Yorkshire, and Henry recalled the story of the day he appeared at school wearing a pair of corduroy shoes, with his wonderful shock of red hair protruding well beyond the bounds of what his namesake, our dear headmaster Henry Bristow, found acceptable.

Henry remembers that he was sent from the school with two and sixpence (30p) to have the offending hairline reduced. Norman remembers an announcement at morning assembly made by the headmaster with regard to declining standards of dress and tidiness, stating that he (the headmaster) had that day sent away from the school a boy who had arrived wearing 'rags on his feet and with hair down to this shoulders' in order that the boy had his hair cut and returned to school wearing acceptable footwear.

Concerned about the length of his own hair, Norman attended the next day with a wonderful, short mop of dark hair. His classmates were in awe of this tidy and acceptable hairstyle and asked how much water Norman had used to achieve this target. However, it had not been water but probably about half a jar of Brylcreem (one of the most popular hairstyling products of the day). It took Norman almost the rest of the school week to scrape it from his head but, on a positive note, there was no chance he would get his head stuck in the school railings.

Returning to Henry, he has told Paul and Norman that on his return to school he had to visit the headmaster, having attended to the disputed footwear and hair-length situation. He also says that he used the water-shortening method and, with the donation of half a crown (30p) from the headmaster, was able to buy a packet of cigarettes. He also confirms that the headmaster was well satisfied with the length of the offending barnet.

Who says we didn't get an education at Sutton High School?

Norman remembers that Henry, for his sins, was one of the class milk monitors and, as such, each day was able to leave morning lessons about ten minutes early to enable preparation for distribution to the other pupils of their daily allocation of the calcium-filled white liquid. Small bottles of about a third of a pint of milk were at that time provided for daily consumption to school pupils. Norman also remembers that although he himself did not aspire to the dizzy milk monitor management heights that Henry did, he appointed himself as an apprentice to his chum and when the milk monitors asked to leave the lesson, Norman, no doubt through a sense of caring and consideration for his fellow pupils and not the fact that he could miss ten minutes of some boring lesson, would leave with them. He has no recollection of ever being challenged with regard to what he considers to be his entrepreneurial action.

Henry was a keen and useful football player and went on to play at a good level in the amateur game. He played for Mechanical Engineering Sports Club and had a brief spell in the Southwestern League; just as in his school days, Henry, as a centre forward, proved a handful for any opponent.

Good on you, Henry.

Sink or Swim

Paul:

The institution that was Sutton High School for Boys was in fact not too far from the well-known part of Plymouth called the Barbican where the Pilgrim Fathers (not the dads of any Argyle players to my knowledge) are reputed to have commenced their travels across the Atlantic on their now well-documented journey of discovery.

So it was that on one particular day, Henry Menyena, two school friends and I accompanied one other individual, who shall remain nameless to preserve his dignity, after deciding that we would spend our lunchtime tracing the historic journey those intrepid explorers had made all those years ago. Well, that's what the nameless classmate was led to believe. I can only assume Norman was at school busily revising for the English GCE O level he was destined not to get.

We arrived at the Barbican, and it was immediately noted that the water seemed quite deep. At that point one of our number, I'm sure it would not have been me, decided that we, as a collective, should ascertain just how deep the water actually was. A volunteer was needed to test our theory that the water was not as deep as it appeared.

Now, our unnamed classmate was quite small in stature. Basically, he was a bit of a 'short-arse', but as he was quite solid, the rest of the group felt he would float much better than any of us. So we volunteered him for the task; despite his protestations, the bespectacled youngster was unceremoniously hoisted in the air with each of us taking either a leg or an arm of the human 'buoy' (yes, I do mean buoy).

As I recall, I grabbed an arm; we then took the unsuspecting soul and swung him to and fro, as if he were some form of human fairground attraction, before launching him like a rocket into the cold harbour water below.

I can confirm that 'humans do float', although school uniforms can shrink if they come into contact with copious amounts of salt water. I am pleased to report that the experiment was a complete success, although when the human guinea pig clambered back amongst us, he did seem a little confused as to where he was; the fact that he flew into the water wearing spectacles but rejoined us minus said 'eye-pieces' probably explained his confusion.

Fortunately, he was able to find his way back to school, but I think for some reason he seemed reluctant to take part in swimming lessons from that day on.

Saturday 30 October 1965

Bristol City v Plymouth Argyle
Division Two – Afternoon Kick Off
Paul:
Went to the game by train – my first away match.

There was a big Argyle following in a crowd of over 17,000. I remember being behind the goal and Bristol battered us. They had big John Atyeo up front with Brian Clark. John Leiper in the Argyle goal had a blinder and we got a 0–0 draw.

I went with George Taylor, a lad called Fred Beer and Tony Weiphright of Weston Mill, another area of Plymouth.

I caught the bug straight away, that feeling of us against the world. This was to be the first of many away trips and great adventures.

George Taylor was a lifelong Argyle fan who sadly passed away two years ago. In those early days everyone knew everyone, and George soon became one of the clique.

Living in Dorchester Avenue, Whitleigh, Plymouth, George ran a local football team called Dorchester Rovers, which Norman and I played for. Naturally our games were on a Sunday so as not to coincide with the Super Greens games.

Secret Operation

Following that historic day on 30 July 1966 (no, that was not when the duo finished school) when England won the World Cup, an English League side, which comprised many of the participants of that momentous July occasion, was due on the 21 September 1966 to play an Irish League side at Home Park.

Well, 'quelle surprise', Norman and Paul considered it only right and proper that they should lend their dual support to the English League side when they trained prior to the game.

So it was that the boys turned up at Home Park to see their heroes. There were just a couple of flaws in their decision; firstly, the game was on a Wednesday, which coincidentally was a school day, but would it be best to invest their time in attending boring lessons, or should they attend a session where they could learn about recent sporting history, something which would stay with them forever?

Well, there they were at Home Park then. Unfortunately, another flaw in their decision making was that they had not realised the training session for the English League was at the Brickfields, a sports ground some two or three miles away and not at the home of the Greens. Another decision to be made – sneak back to school or go to the Brickfields?

So, there they we were at the Brickfields, watching the likes of Bobby Moore, Martin Peters and Geoff Hurst (now Sir Geoff Hurst). It was, for us youngsters, a magnificent and memorable experience; the two of us may have appeared on local television that night. We would have been the ones hiding our faces whilst looking away from the camera. Well, what the headmaster of our school couldn't see he didn't need to bother about, wouldn't you agree?

Incidentally, the English League won the game 12–0 in front of a crowd of more than 35,000.

Lion Tamers

Norman:

I am at The Den, Millwall, on 14 January 1967, feeling perhaps a little nervous at being in this infamous football stadium in the Docklands, East London. Still, little old Argyle wouldn't provide any problems for a side that had gone fifty-nine matches at home without defeat; surely us Janners (the nickname for Plymothians) would be perfectly safe in that welcoming hotbed of football.

At this point in that season, Argyle had failed to win away in the old Division Two; clearly, we would have no chance of winning this one. How wrong can you be? I remember that John Mitten made his Argyle debut that day and we won the game; yes, we won the game, 2–1. (The only other away game we won that season was a 2–1 victory at Bolton on 22 April 1967 with John Hore and Alan Banks the Argyle goal scorers).

I remember beating a rather hasty retreat some ten to fifteen minutes prior to the conclusion of the game, just in case we actually won and some of the opposition fans may have felt that they should invite me to some local hostelry to celebrate in convivial fashion the success of the team from Devon.

I am not convinced that I really felt they would be quite that contrite in defeat, so basically, I legged it!

I remember later reports of Peter Shearing (who was in goal for Argyle that day) walking from the field of play with missiles being thrown at him; I think his performance was so good that he could probably have caught most of them and thrown them back.

I believe the team coach was attacked and damaged and so with the benefit of hindsight, I am sure that my retreat strategy towards the end of the game that day was perfectly justified.

Incidentally, the goal scorers for Argyle that day were Mike Bickle and Alan Banks. The Lions Tamed!

Two Greens in a Red Forest

So, what a great draw for the Argyle, then in the old Division Two, away to Division One (then the top English Division), Nottingham Forest in round three of the FA Cup. Harty and Norm, of course, had to go and show their support. There was a football special train; the lads were still attendees of that fine institution of educational prowess, namely Sutton High School for Boys, so no problem for a Saturday afternoon kick-off on 28 January 1967.

Now, as true Argyle supporters, and that was what the dynamic duo clearly were, it was, they felt, imperative that the good folk of Nottingham realised that the boys from Plymouth would be in town. So, notwithstanding that the legend that was Robin Hood is said to have cavorted around the Nottingham area, ironically wearing Lincoln green when he apparently stole from the rich to give to the poor, the two perhaps slightly naïve boys from Janner Land felt that they too should turn up in costume and that maybe they could encourage the Argyle to steal this cup tie from the then Division One giants and give it to the poor (in football terms, anyway) supporters from Devon.

Not content with the traditional regalia of the football fan, Paul wore a sports jacket with Plymouth Argyle sewn on its back in green wool whilst Norman had a brown suede-type jacket (that had been rescued from the bin after his mother had dispatched it to said receptacle), which had Plymouth Argyle emblazoned on its back in white paint; not much doubt who they were supporting then. Whilst being very keen and loyal fans, the boys did decline to wear green tights.

The game took place in the fair city of Nottingham at the City Ground on the banks of the River Trent. Argyle held out for the best part of sixty minutes and then Jimmy Bloomfield scored to put the Greens 1–0 up; could the smash-and-grab raid be on? Forest equalised; a draw would have made us happy with a replay at Home Park. Sadly, it was not to be, for our illustrious opponents scored again, 2–1, and then our wonderful Barrie Jones missed a great opportunity to square the tie when he shot over the bar.

Barrie Jones was a great player who was signed by Argyle for £45,000 from Swansea, which for the Greens was a club record fee at that time and was, when he signed in 1964, a British record fee for a winger.

The boys left the City Ground with their team defeated but by no means disgraced, safe in the realisation that Argyle had given Forest and their fans quite a scare. So it was that the duo happily proceeded along the dark wintry streets of Nottingham, making their way back to get their train home, mingling with many Argyle and Forest fans from the 34,000 or so crowd. As they headed along the road, they became aware that some of the natives were not particularly friendly; in fact, they seemed to be hunting for scalps. The boys' hair at the time was of reasonable length and they rather wanted to keep it that way.

They soon realised that they were in danger of being hunted down and also realised that the two of them had become isolated from the relative security of being in a big group of Argyle fans. More importantly, they also remembered that rather than blending in with the crowd of Forest fans, they might as well have been lit up by a dozen floodlights, for of course there they were, with their jackets advertising the wonderful Plymouth Argyle! The team from down south who had so nearly embarrassed the first division giants.

Norman recalls the following:

I remember a very kind man, presumably one of the more benevolent Forest fans, saying to the baying gang, 'Leave them alone,' and telling us to keep moving. As my amigo and I were approached by the gang, we feared the worst. I was wearing a green and white scarf, which had been given to me by Paul's brother Phil. (Phil has since alleged that the scarf was brand new and never previously worn, and that it was removed from his bedroom by Paul without Phil's knowledge.) The scarf was grabbed from me and, fearing for our safety, both of us took the decision to run! We disappeared into some even darker backstreets to escape the mob; we were still wearing our mobile advertising jackets, but fortunately we escaped and made our way back to catch the train.

Of course, we were severely traumatised by the experience; well, that's the rationale we used when deciding on the return journey to Plymouth that we would be unable to attend school the following Monday. Paul was obviously more traumatised than me and failed to turn up at school until the Tuesday afternoon.

Clearly in those days the sort of trauma that the two of us claimed as the reason for non-attendance was not accepted; in fact, we were (probably in our opinion only) subjected to further trauma in that we were each given our own private detentions on a one-to-one basis with a teacher each, the tariff used being one detention for every lesson we had missed, but a small price to pay for the love of the Greens. We are sure you will agree.

A Fitting Experience

Norman:

So, I left the hallowed halls of what at that time, I believe, was considered to be one of the two top boys' grammar schools in Plymouth, the other being Devonport High School for Boys, which probably to us boys from Sutton was a rival establishment, which we would have considered second-class compared to us. I suppose a rivalry which might not be much different to the love and affection that an Argyle fan might (or might not) feel for a team some forty miles or so up the road from the Theatre of Greens, of which more later. Mind you, the predominant colours of Devonport High School were green and white.

Anyway, I digress. I left school with the grand sum of zero GCE O levels (unlike my pal Paul, who did get one, an English O level; I'm not bitter mind you, but I have often thought I should have had that English O level). Perhaps I spelled my name incorrectly on the exam paper; I guess I will never know. What I will say is Hart is a much easier name to spell than Foweraker.

Well, the dockyard seemed to be the way forward; I actually passed an entrance exam and so it was that with some trepidation I entered the world of work. I became a Fitter and Turner apprentice in the dockyard. I think I realised quite quickly that this was not where my future in the workplace lay. I thought I would be working on engines, fitting out war ships and the like, and perhaps that would have been the case several years down the line, but filing pieces of metal until they were perfectly flat, checking the job on a surface plate, using a micrometre which measured thousandths of an inch, then taking the job to an instructor, who would say something like, 'Not bad, boy, just file down a little high spot and that should be fine,' only to take it back again with the realisation that it was worse than on the previous occasion was to say the least soul destroying. So, after about eighteen months, I was released with my mother's permission from the apprenticeship.

I moved on to work in an office role with a transport company named Drake Carriers, then on to Rank Bush Murphy at Ernesettle, Plymouth in the Goods Department. I was probably now becoming a little more interested in my future direction of travel. I don't know why but the police service came into my thoughts. I am unsure if at that time I thought of it as a career path; maybe I felt it was a form of escapism (very apt for a potential police officer). Whatever the reason, at the age of about twenty-two I became a boy in blue and after my initial training was posted to Exeter, but my love of Argyle meant that I would always be Green at Heart.

'Swilly Boy' – Police Constable Norman Foweraker

Ice-Cold Decision

Norman:

As I often say to my darling wife, you should not let football rule your life and as it may now be realised, I am a man well versed in the art of compromise.

Many years ago, in my amateur football days, there was the need (well, that's my story and I'm sticking to it) for me to turn out for my team who, from memory, were Tamar Athletic. So here was another difficult problem: at that time, I had a temporary job as a mobile purveyor of many different varieties of ice-cold dairy products, AKA an ice-cream man.

I was to many 'Mr Carmello', often to be seen driving an ageing vehicle around various Plymouth locations, supposedly to the tune of *The Third Man* (for those of you of a certain age – the Harry Lime theme tune); however, some of the chimes were missing from the chime box and because of the unholy row that came from the loud speaker as a result, it was much easier to just ring a bell.

Returning to my footballing predicament, I could not let the rest of the team down, so I compromised and made a decision. I enlisted the help of my unsuspecting mother and took her on a trip to the Southway/Tamerton area of Plymouth, parking the ice-cream van close to where coincidentally my team were due to play their game.

How fortunate that I happened to have my football gear on board as well as a ready-made ice-cream salesperson. So, compromise was achieved. I did not let the team down and my 'mater' was able to supervise ice-cream sales.

Thanks, Mum.

Gutted

It's Wednesday 14 August 1968 and Argyle have been drawn at home to 'you know who' (Exeter City, Argyle's main Devon rivals, if you don't know who) in the first round of the Football League Cup, as it was then known.

Should be a simple enough job to dispatch the opposition from up the A38, then move on to a nice round two fixture, but no; whilst Pat Dunne kept a clean sheet in the home game, Peter Shearing (who incidentally had joined Argyle from Exeter in 1966 only to return to the dark side in July of 1968) was equally secure in the Exeter goal. The game finished 0–0 so it was off to St James's Park, Exeter on Wednesday 21 August for the replay.

Norman believes that Argyle fans were housed in the Big Bank End of the ground because of their large following. Yet again, the game finished goalless, on this occasion following the obligatory period of extra time.

How was this matter going to be resolved? Well, in those days it would seem, proverbially speaking, it was a fight to the finish. So it was that on the evening of Monday 26 August, the contest was scheduled to resume at Plainmoor, the home of Torquay United.

Now, as this was an evening kick off on a weekday, Paul and Norman would have to make the short journey after their day of toil. Norman was the dedicated driver on this occasion and in view of the time of day and the volume of support from Plymouth, traffic en route to the game was, to say the least, congested and with the mighty duo being concerned about arriving late for the game, it became necessary for drastic action to be taken, and a manoeuvre to overtake a rather long line of vehicles to ensure prompt arrival at the aforementioned Plainmoor, in the opinion of the two, became necessary.

Norman was clearly in complete control of the situation, although the pair do believe that there could have been the odd gesture or two from other motorists who were possibly indicating that Argyle were going to win 2–0 (presumably that's what they were gesturing!). Norman can't be sure but wondered not for the first time if Paul could have been wearing khaki trousers.

All of their efforts to reach the match on time ultimately proved to be in vain as, about one minute from the end of extra time in this second replay, Exeter's John Kirkham scored what was the winning goal to take his side through to a round two home tie against Sheffield Wednesday, then of the old First Division.

I don't know about Paul, remembers Norman, but I recall being close to tears as I stood in disbelief watching red and white being displayed in victorious manner. How could our arch-rivals have beaten the mighty Greens? But it had happened and to add to the pain, Exeter went on to beat Sheffield Wednesday 3–1 before eventually losing 6–3 away to Spurs in the third round.

Well done, Exeter, you must have been good to defeat the Greens, but why oh why couldn't it have been us?

Incidentally, Paul's brother Phil also attended this game but travelled on one of the supporters' coaches; at the end of the game, Paul and Norman went in a different direction to Phil; however, Phil recalls rejoining the couple to tell them about some trouble he had witnessed.

Phil recounts this story later in the book along with some other random memories.

Real In-Tent

Norman:

I don't think Paul was ever a boy scout, recounts Norman, and I was a member of the Boys Brigade. I'm not convinced that either of us learned very much about the art of tying knots or pitching a tent, but there shouldn't be much of a problem with this camping business, surely!

So it was that the buddies decided that a camping holiday was such a great idea for the two young men. It would be a great adventure, particularly if they went 'up north' where they would be able to take in some football matches. Well, 'quelle surprise' (why didn't I get O level French?).

Argyle were due to play at Southport on Saturday 6 September 1969, but on Saturday 30 August, Everton (from the city of Liverpool) were at home to Leeds. So, what a great summer holiday for the likely pair.

I was now a driver with vehicle, so off we went with the car loaded full of the necessary gear for the camping adventure, staying in the Blackpool area from where, of course, we could access, quite easily, both Liverpool and Southport.

Now, Paul claims that with our limited experience in the camping arena, the situation when us guys attempted to erect our canvas abode was, to say the least, tense; in fact, he alleges we almost came to blows – as if! Well, that's my version and I'm sticking to it.

I think after our comedic attempts to erect our tent, peace finally broke out and we settled into our holiday.

I remember reading a headline in a newspaper prior to the Everton v Leeds game where Jack Charlton stated: 'We don't fear Everton.' In the event, Paul and I witnessed a magnificent game of football at Everton's Goodison Park, which was played in front of a crowd of over 53,000. Everton won 3–2, having been 3–0 up, with goals from Joe Royal (two) and Jimmy Husband, and with goals from Billy

Bremner and Allan Clarke (nicknamed Sniffer) for Leeds; we feel we were privileged to see two teams who went on to finish first and second in what was then Division One, with Everton finishing as champions and Leeds as runners up.

On our way back home the following week, we went to watch the mighty Greens play out a dull 0–0 draw at Southport in front of a crowd with an attendance of less than 3,500. But hey, we were, are and always will be Argyle fans and to see our team in action that day was as special to us as the magnificent spectacle at Goodison the previous week. Incidentally, Southport were relegated that season whilst Argyle finished in seventeenth place behind (would you believe) Torquay, who finished thirteenth. Come on you Greens (COYG)!

Saturday 1 November 1969
Barrow v Plymouth Argyle
Division Three – 3.15 pm Kick Off
Paul:
I was working by now and had passed my driving test, which meant every away game was a possibility. My mate Norman and I would buy old cars and take turns in driving to the games.

It was Norman's turn to drive to Barrow, and four of us (myself, Norman, Mike Cannicott and Mike Wallace) set off about 7.00 pm on the Friday night. We didn't have the use of motorways as we do nowadays, just a series of A roads and ring roads. With only one person driving, it took ages to get there. I remember seeing a Welcome to the Lake District sign and thought: we can't be far away now. Two hours later we arrived in Barrow; it had taken seventeen hours to get there.

We were fast becoming familiar faces on the away circuit and were usually given complimentary tickets to the games. The team seemed amazed to see us waiting for them at the players' entrance.

The game itself was pretty dire; it was a horrible day in a poor ground. Argyle drew 1–1 and Steve Davey scored for us. We saw the players leave after the game before contemplating the drive home.

Sleep was a necessity, particularly for the driver, so we decided to leave Barrow, find somewhere to eat and park up for a few hours. The driver (Norman) slept for hours, and we stopped numerous times on the way back, finally arriving in Plymouth at about 8.00 pm on the Sunday evening.

It was work on the Monday and my turn to drive next time. I think we were the pioneers of 'miles and miles and miles to follow the Greens'.

Norman:

My beloved and I have been fortunate enough to travel to New Zealand more than once, a distance of some 11,500 miles from England, and the journey time to Barrow with the four usual suspects (the two Mikes, Paul and me), in what I would have at the time considered to be my pristine used vehicle, probably took us almost as long as our journeys to the other side of the world and was almost certainly more precarious, possibly due to the fact that I was the only pilot for our expedition. Retrospectively I think I should ask myself how I managed to draw such a short straw prior to the trip. Why not Torquay, or even a trip up the A38? The answer is clear – for love of those 'Greens'.

I think by the time we reached Barrow, matchsticks to keep my eyes wide open would not have gone amiss.

As Paul has mentioned, the game ended in a 1–1 draw and the long and arduous drive home would have involved copious amounts of sleep (not, I hasten to add, whilst driving).

The journey was long; the game, as Paul has described it, was 'dire': Why did we do it? Two-word answer – 'It's Argyle.'

Should We Go or Should We Stay?

Paul:

It was a cold day on Tuesday 25 November 1969; I was determined to go to Gillingham where the Super Greens were due to play the following evening in a Division Three fixture with a kick off scheduled for 7.30 pm. I had already asked Norman if he would join me on this winter wonderland adventure but he refused my hitchhiking proposal point blank; however, he did say he would go if I took my 'stretch limo' (AKA my trusted old Austin A35).

Due to my strained economic situation (I was skint), I decided that I would go ahead and hitchhike alone. I got myself as far as Marsh Mills (on the outskirts of Plymouth) where I remained raising my 'freezing thumb' for what seemed like an eternity, at which point I decided I would return to my beloved mother, collect my car and go to Norman's home, which by then was in Devonport, and surprise him by saying, 'Get your coat, we are going.'

Norman:

By now it was probably about 10 pm on the said Tuesday. There was a sharp rap on the door. Polly, the family parrot (obviously still sporting her Argyle green colours) screeched, 'Who's that? Who's that?' I answered the door to find Paul standing there, ready for us to make the long journey to Gillingham.

A quick exchange between me and my bemused and somewhat annoyed (to say the least) mother then took place where I explained how unwell I was feeling, asking her to contact my employers the next day. I would have asked Polly our parrot to make the call but I don't think she had the right phone number.

Paul did the driving through the night, stopping only for some rest before we arrived in Chatham (close to Gillingham) in time for some breakfast. We then had the day to explore the area before making the short journey to

Gillingham. What we soon realised was that just about everything in the area closed early on Wednesdays' and so we went to the ground and arrived at Priestfield in the early afternoon. A very kind official of the club invited us to look around the ground. I recall Paul and I standing in the away end goalmouth and one of us saying something like: 'This is where, tonight, Pat Dunne will tip the ball over the crossbar, helping us to a famous away victory.'

In the event, after receiving complimentary tickets from the players, Paul and I sat in a freezing cold stand, watching Argyle get 'hammered' in a 4–0 defeat before we made the arduous return journey to Plymouth. Was it worth it? Should we have stayed or gone? No question about it; it was Argyle and, of course, we had to go.

Funding our Passion:
Paul remembers we could never be classed as entrepreneurs but as far as Argyle were concerned, there were no lengths we would not go to in order to follow the Greens. We were both fortunate enough to have jobs. Norman worked for Drake Carriers (after leaving the dockyard) in the Administration department and I worked for Tecalemit Group Services, also coincidentally in admin. Naturally both jobs involved working Monday to Friday; after all, we would never have worked on a Saturday, would we?

Paul continues: When I left school, my dear mother was determined I would get a job. There was no way she would let me become a 'beach bum', my preferred choice. It wasn't too long before my mother announced she had managed to get me an interview at Debenhams Department Store, Plymouth working in the Menswear department. I was mortified! Debenhams; they opened on a Saturday, didn't they? I was adamant that I would not attend that interview. The situation was now serious; I had to find a job quickly. It was then that I joined Tecalemit Group

Services as a post boy. In those days people were paid weekly in cash and I was to receive £4.00 from which I would give my mother £2.00 per week.

What a result; Mum was happy and I was free to travel the country following Argyle. What a shock I was to have when I received my first pay packet. It was a little brown envelope and I could see pound notes folded inside; I was also aware that there was loose money. *Something is wrong*, I thought. I was told I would receive £4.00 per week; it was only then that I was to learn about deductions. They had robbed me of seven shillings and six pence (just over 37p today) and now I only had three pounds, twelve shillings and six pence (today just over 62p) to play with. How was I to know about national insurance and so on? I had agreed to give my mother two pounds a week; what was I to do?

There was no way I could afford to go to away games on one pound, twelve shillings and six pence (about 1.62p today). This is where the entrepreneurial bit kicks in. As a school boy, I did a paper round which included morning and evening collections and also Sunday mornings. The paperman always had difficulty in finding someone to sell newspapers from Mutley Plain, an area not far from my home in Penlee Place. So, a few weeks later, I was selling Sunday papers on Mutley Plain from outside the Dewhurst butcher shop and guess what I was being paid? Seven shillings and six pence a week (just over 37p), still a little short but enough for me to follow the Greens.

Life was sweet and I was able to continue travelling miles and miles and miles to follow the greens.

Norman:

Paul is absolutely right. Our pockets were always full for the finest things in our lives, and at that time that was following our heroes around the country, and in order to fund our escapades, it was necessary to make sacrifices in other areas.

One such occasion for me was when working at Drake Carriers, I took a fancy to a young colleague of the opposite sex and since I had my limousine – well, at the time I think it may have been my old Austin A35 (quite possibly a collector's item now) – I thought, *One day, I'll offer my colleague a lift home. That will impress her, and who knows what may develop from there?* I think she lived in the Plymstock area of Plymouth, so quite a long bus ride home for her. The offer of a lift was made and accepted; great, I thought. In she got and off we went. Now, in order to reserve finances to fund trips to see the mighty Greens in action, fuel consumption for routine matters such as getting to and from work needed to be addressed. On my journey towards Plymstock with the young lady beside me, suitably impressed, I felt, I made the discovery that the internal combustion engine needed the not-so-secret ingredient of petrol and does not run on air. We got as far as the Embankment, a short distance from our workplace at Marsh Mills, when the car spluttered and coughed and ran out of the aforementioned petrol. Needless to say, the ignominy of the girl having to catch the bus home and me red faced searching for a garage to obtain some fuel meant that any thoughts of a romance disappeared on a red bus to Plymstock, but at least I would be able to afford my continued love affair with the Argyle.

I do remember visiting Harty on some Sundays on Mutley Plain where he would be doing his static paper round; after all, it would have been essential to support him in his quest for extra funding to enable our joint priority and, no doubt, to analyse and dissect the previous day's game. HAPPY DAYS.

Saturday 13 December 1969

Halifax Town v Plymouth Argyle
Division Three – Afternoon Kick Off
Paul:
Three weeks after hitchhiking to an away match at Doncaster, it was back to Yorkshire again with a trip to Halifax, this time by minibus. What could go wrong?

Ten of us set off at 9 pm on the Friday evening from Home Park, including Mike Cannicott and Mike Wallace. I didn't really know the others and hadn't met the driver before. He wasn't a football fan, but had offered to drive the bus if we all covered his costs. He had family in the area whom he intended to visit.

We arrived in Halifax at about 7.30 am on the morning of the game; we all stayed together and soon found a café and tucked into a full English. Mike Wallace suffered from epilepsy and sure enough he had a fit during breakfast. I had never witnessed one before but I can distinctly remember him shaking violently for ages before crumbling to the floor, taking the tablecloth and half the breakfasts with him. The café owner went mad and wanted us all out. Someone explained that Mike could not be moved until he had fully recovered. Thankfully he did.

After breakfast, the group gradually dispersed and the two Mikes and I wandered around Halifax with not a home fan in sight. We arrived at the ground, called the Shay, in plenty of time to meet the players and receive our complimentary tickets. We then took our seats in the grandstand.

Argyle were woeful that day and lost 2–0. Derek Rickard made his debut but, in my opinion, that game is up there with one of the worst Argyle performances ever.

We were due to be picked up at 7.30 pm from the Shay to return home. Half past seven came and went and no driver. Some of the lads had left their coats on the bus and were shivering from the cold. It was two weeks before Christmas in Yorkshire and freezing. Somehow, and I don't remember how, word got to us that our driver was not picking us up until 7.30 am the next morning (Sunday). Panic set in; we were stranded.

In those days, the Shay wasn't fully locked, and we decided to sleep in the grandstand; however, sleep was virtually impossible on the stone-cold floor in the main stand. I think the fact we were all moving around trying to stay warm alerted someone to our presence because at around 3 am the police arrived and we were all taken to the police station for questioning. Eventually they believed us and we spent the rest of the night in the cells (not locked) in Halifax Police Station, with hot drinks being supplied.

We were back at the Shay at seven thirty in the morning. The driver eventually arrived at about 8 am and swore blind that that was the arrangement. I never knew him and have never seen him since; at least there were no more away games before Christmas.

A Knockout on Boxing Day

Friday 26 December 1969

Plymouth Argyle v Torquay

Division Three – Afternoon Kick Off

Norman:

A crowd in excess of 17,000 witnessed a supremely confident performance from the lowly Pilgrims against their high-riding (yes, you read it right) opponents from the English Riviera, Torquay United.

United came to the game in fourth position in the old Division Three, whilst Argyle were languishing in twentieth place, just one point above the dreaded drop zone.

What was to follow during this Boxing Day encounter between two Devon teams, whose rivalry perhaps hasn't always been as fierce as that between the 'Greens and the Reds', was nevertheless both surprising and, dare I say, humiliating for the Yellows of Torquay.

Argyle won 6–0 with Mike Bickle scoring four and Norman Piper two.

After the game, I recall that Paul and I went to the Players' Entrance at Home Park to congratulate our players.

When Torquay's rugged defender, Billy Kitchener, whose role was to try and stop Mike Bickle from scoring, exited the ground, Paul could not resist saying, 'How did you get on today, Billy, and how many did Mike Bickle score?'

I'm not sure Paul was aware of any possible reply since he was probably last seen 'legging it' across Central Park (the large park in which Home Park is situated), fearful of having his undoubtedly good looks rearranged by the big man from the English Riviera.

Paul:

Little did I know at that time that in years to come I would become great friends with the now late Mike Bickle and his partner Sandra.

My friendship with Mike developed when Sandra insisted on washing the kit of the ex-Argyle Players Team, then known as the Argyle Legends, following a charity game at Weston Mill in 2013. For the next ten years or so, Sandra washed, dried and repaired our various kits. Over many visits to their family home to both deliver and collect the kit, I was usually invited in for a cuppa and a biscuit. 'Yes, I'll have a quick cuppa,' I would reply, then two, sometimes three hours later I would say, 'I really must go now.'

I loved chatting to Mike: he was quiet, shy and shunned the limelight, but over the years he opened up and told me some great stories about his time at Argyle. I would update him as to what his former teammates were currently doing and he would tell me stories about their escapades at Argyle.

Mike sadly passed away in November 2023, just before his eightieth birthday. You can only imagine how proud I was to be asked to speak at his funeral.

RIP, Mike; you truly were the King.

Mike was later to be inducted as an Argyle Icon into Forever Green, but that's another story.

Never Chicken Out Before a Game

Paul:

This tale began on Friday 6 February 1970 before a double-header, Rochdale away on the Saturday and Barnsley away on the Monday night.

In those days I used to go to all the away games and I had been known to buy an old car, which would last about a month, to drive to a couple of away games, or else hitchhike. For this Saturday/Monday combo, my mate Mike Cannicott and I decided on the latter option.

The favourite starting point back then was the London Inn at Ivybridge, a few miles east of Plymouth, where you were guaranteed to catch traffic going north. For this trip we had decided to take a tent and would find somewhere to sleep.

As usual, we were dropped at the London Inn at about 7 pm on the Friday night; the weather was bitterly cold. Within half an hour, a car had stopped; it turned out it was going all the way to Crewe. After a couple of brief stops, we arrived in the Cheshire town at about 5 am. Four hours later, we were still in the same place, thumbing a lift. Not to be deterred, we decided to catch a train to Rochdale and arrived there at about midday.

As always, we went straight to the ground, waited for the team coach to arrive, then chatted to the players and received our complimentary tickets from them as was often the case.

Of the two matches, Argyle were expected to beat Rochdale but Barnsley was going to be a difficult game. Sat in the grandstand at Rochdale's home ground, Spotland, we were wondering where we would pitch our tent that night. Snow was falling and I can't recall any other Argyle fans being there. In those days, Argyle's away record was atrocious (I only saw them win twelve times in over a hundred away games) and needless to say we lost 2–1, with Derek Rickard scoring for Argyle.

Throughout the game we had been chatting to a middle-aged Rochdale supporter, who was amazed at our dedication. Towards the end of the game, he asked where we were staying on the Saturday and Sunday. When we explained our plans, he was horrified, saying we would probably die from frostbite by the morning. He then kindly offered to put us up for two nights on his chicken farm. Apparently, all we had to do was clean the chicken pens on the Sunday to earn our keep. We arrived at this farm, in the middle of nowhere, to be accommodated in a hut in a field. After a hot meal and warm drink, we settled down for the night on a camp bed.

The following morning, we were awakened by the farmer's wife who was carrying a delicious-looking fried breakfast; she said we would need it considering the work that was in store for us. What followed was the hardest and scariest experience I have ever had. The chicken pens were massive and our job was to clear out all the muck, put it into a wheelbarrow, then walk along thin planks and tip the contents off the edge of a hill.

After about twenty trips to and fro, it happened! Walking down the ramp with the wheelbarrow, a gust of wind blew me sideways right off the planks and into the muck below. There was so much of it that I was immediately up to my chest and I thought I was going to sink even deeper. If my mate and the farmer hadn't been there to pull me out, I think I would have disappeared – intervention by Norman into Paul's story: 'In my opinion, that could only happen to Paul. It has been said by some people that you are always in it; it's just the depth that varies – back to you, Paul!'

Paul continues: As the farmer hadn't allowed us into his house beforehand, there was no way he was letting us in now, but what followed was amazing. The farmer got what I can only describe as a large beer barrel and filled it with hot water for me to wash in. The only problem was my clothes; they were filthy and stinking. The farmer's wife said she would dry them out in another hut so that they would be ready for Monday morning – question from Norman: 'So what did you wear for the rest of Sunday?' – back to Paul again.

On the Monday morning, the farmer dropped us off at Rochdale bus station where we caught a bus all the way to Barnsley. My clothes had been cleaned and dried, although my jacket was still rather smelly. When we arrived in Barnsley, the weather was really bad and there was some doubt amongst the locals as to whether the game would be played.

We arrived at the ground at about 5 pm and thankfully were told the game was on. Again, we were given complimentary tickets and Argyle were brilliant that night – winning 1–0 thanks to an early Derek Rickard goal. The defence had been superb all evening and we were ecstatic at the result. After the game, we went to the Players' Entrance to wish them all the best and a safe journey home. Whilst we were there, the police advised us that once the Argyle coach had gone over Snake Pass into Lancashire, the road would be closed.

It was then, completely out of the blue, that one of the Argyle team, Johnny Hore, asked us how we were getting back to Plymouth. When we told him we were hitchhiking, he told us to hang on for a moment. Unbeknown to us, he asked Billy Bingham, Argyle's then manager, if we could travel back on the team coach. What ensued was like a fairy tale.

We couldn't believe it – Billy Bingham had said yes! The team was staying in Stockport overnight and we could sleep on the coach, then travel back to Plymouth with the team on the Tuesday. Can you imagine what two eighteen-year-olds were feeling, being on the team coach with all our heroes? The journey to Stockport was brilliant. I remember sitting near the back of the coach watching my hero, Mike Bickle, playing cards with Fred Molyneux, Dave Lean and several others, but I had to explain the reason for my smelly jacket. Then, when we arrived at Stockport, the players fetched blankets for us to use whilst we slept overnight on the coach.

The following morning, in return for some breakfast that was smuggled out to us, we were asked to find a chemist as one of the players was suffering from catarrh. I don't remember too much about the journey home; I think I slept most of the way, but I do remember the coach manoeuvring around the streets of Plymouth, dropping the players off. My mate and I were off loaded at Home Park. I couldn't wait to tell all my friends; what a weekend!

That 1969/70 season, I went to every away game and saw Argyle win six times, but on numerous occasions I was one of a few Argyle fans at the games. We ended up finishing sixteenth in Division Three.

Other highlights of that season were to Barrow and back in an Austin A35, to Mansfield in a Ford Popular, Doncaster where we walked around the Gloucester ring road, Gillingham on a Wednesday night in November where we lost 4–0 and the car broke down, and Leyton Orient where I wrote the car off on the journey. We still made the game, but that's another story… Come on you Greens!

Sterling Hart

Friday 27 March 1970 – Orient v Argyle
11 am – Kick Off
Saturday 28 March 1970 – Bury v Argyle
Paul:
The plan for this double-header was simple.
I was to drive to Orient for the Good Friday morning game and then it was up to Bury for the Easter Saturday game.

The usual four suspects, Norman, Mike Cannicott, Mike Wallace and I, set off in my Austin A35 late on the Thursday evening (the total engine power was less than 1,000 cc). It was a foul night, lashing with rain. We were travelling on the old A30, approaching Fenny Bridges near Honiton, Devon, chatting away when Norman said something about some new trousers he had on. I had a look, no more than a glance, and the bridge was upon us; we were now heading straight towards the offside of the road. It was an S bend and I swung the steering wheel to the left, right and left again and we went over and over, numerous times before landing upside down in a ditch.

There was what seemed to be an endless silence. I knew I was alright, but nobody said anything. Then Mike Cannicott whispered: 'Is everyone OK?' One by one we said we were; the only way out was through the rear window where the glass had come out whole. We clambered out to see the car upside down, acid flowing out of the battery; thankfully the ditch was out of the way of oncoming traffic.

To this day I will never forget Mike saying: 'OK, chiefs, let's turn the car back over and we will be on our way.' The A35 was built like a tank, thank goodness, but there was no way we were going anywhere in that. The police had arrived by now and took statements from us all. At the time we were all fine and insisted we wanted to get to London. We told them that supporters' coaches were travelling that night and the police somehow organised one of the coaches to pick us up. There were no spare seats, but we were happy to sit on the floor.

En route to London we discovered the supporters' coach trip was planning to take in the Tottenham v Nottingham Forest game in the afternoon after watching Argyle at Orient in the morning. Meanwhile, the police were informing our parents about the accident and saying we were all safe.

We eventually got to Brisbane Road (the home ground of Orient) and Argyle, not for the first time that season, were awful and were hammered 4–1. Then it was off to White Hart Lane (the then home ground of Tottenham Hotspur) and another 4–1, this time to Spurs.

On the way home, still sat on the floor of the coach, shock was beginning to sink in and by the time we arrived back in Plymouth, I was a wreck.

So instead of being at Bury on the Saturday, where incidentally Argyle lost 3–1, I was ill in bed and felt unwell for days. My poor mother had to go to Honiton with Norman to sort out the car. Apparently, the damage was so bad that the garage believed if we had gone over one more time, the roof would have caved in. To make matters worse, I only had third party, fire and theft insurance; it cost £8.00 to tow the car to the garage and as the car was a write-off, I only received £7.50 from the insurance company.

Norman:

Yes, I also have fairly vivid recall of that fateful day when Paul, the Mikes, Cannicott and Wallace, and I merrily made our way along the A30, heading for the first of two away fixtures. I know the area of carriageway where Harty performed his act of 'daring do' reasonably well now. I note with some scepticism my chum's assertion that he was merely and briefly addressing a fashion observation which I had allegedly made concerning my strides, rather than suggesting that maybe there was perhaps a little over steer on the part of our driver, with his swinging to the left, to the right and to the left as he attempted a Formula One manoeuvre in what essentially was something a little smaller both in size and power than an old-style Robin Reliant three-wheeled vehicle.

Having said that, the strength of the chassis of that vehicle undoubtedly warded off a more catastrophic event. We disentangled ourselves from the pile of scrap, which was what the vehicle was by now, even though I think Mike Cannicott felt we could straighten it up and carry on. Mike, I recall, realising the car was not going to be repaired by the roadside, suggested, 'Right then, what are we going to do? Hitch?' Oh, the innocence and naivety of us young Greens.

I think Paul felt that this was a case of the bridge that moved and he thinks that as I was in the front seat, maybe I should have done something to halt the dramatic incursion of the mighty brickwork structure.

Some days later I visited the garage to which the vehicle had been taken with Mrs H, Paul's mum; it was a write-off and like Paul at that time, a wreck, but thankfully we all survived to tell the tale.

Saturday 3 February 1973

Leeds United v Plymouth Argyle

FA Cup – Fourth Round – 3 pm Kick Off

Paul:

After beating Middlesborough in the third round of the FA Cup, Argyle got the plum draw in round four, cup holders Leeds United at Elland Road, Leeds.

For this game I was doing it in the civilised way. Tecalemit Garage Equipment, where I worked, had organised a coach and match tickets, so it made perfect sense to travel with them.

On arriving at the ground, I couldn't help but be overawed by the sheer size of it. The atmosphere was rapidly building with thousands of Argyle fans already there. We passed the supporters' club bar and asked if we could go in; to our surprise they said yes. The Leeds fans in the club were brilliant. After all, we were little Plymouth Argyle and it was obvious they were expecting an easy game. We had a few drinks before heading off to find our way into the ground. If their fans were nice in the club, all that changed once inside the stadium.

It was the most hostile and intimidating crowd I'd ever seen. The attendance that day was almost 39,000. Argyle, though, were magnificent that afternoon, every one of them. When Derek Rickard scored a fantastic header for Argyle, from a pinpoint Davie Provan cross, to equalise, I thought the miracle was on. Leeds had other ideas and Mick Bates scored soon after to settle it.

I remember we went into the city centre after the game for a Chinese and now the game was won, the majority of Leeds fans were once again brilliant towards us. We had a great night out in Leeds, although with one or two scary moments, before boarding our coach for home. The Tony Waiters Argyle managerial revolution was just beginning.

Leeds went on to the final again only to be beaten by Sunderland, whose team contained a certain Micky Horswill (later to become an Argyle favourite).

It was one of those great occasions where I can say: 'I was there.'

As a footnote, this 2–1 defeat of Argyle was my 112th away game since 1964 and I had only seen us win nine times.

Santos

Wednesday 14 March 1973
Plymouth Argyle v Santos
Friendly - 7.30 pm Kick Off
Paul:

Had the day off work for this one. After all, it's not every day that Pele comes to town. It had been a busy few days leading up to the game; Swansea away on the Saturday and then joining the thousands queuing for tickets for hours on the Sunday. No exaggeration; there were literally thousands, and there were times when we wondered if tickets would run out before we got to the kiosk.

On the day of the game, word got out that Santos were travelling down by train and arriving in Plymouth mid-afternoon. As I have previously mentioned, I had been collecting autographs for a number of years and so I thought I'd try for Pele. North Road Station was chaotic and it was hopeless as the players were ushered onto a waiting coach for a pre-match meal at the Holiday Inn.

A trip to the hotel also proved unsuccessful. There were too many people around so I thought I would 'leg it' to the ground nice and early and try again. When Santos arrived at Home Park, it was mad; Pele was escorted to the Players' Entrance by the police and he stopped only to sign one autograph. I was so close I thought I was going to get him, but it was one autograph and away he went.

I made my way into the Devonport end and joined my mates behind the goal. The atmosphere was unbelievable as the two teams took to the field. Nobody at that stage was aware that the game nearly didn't take place.

Realising that there was a huge crowd in the ground, Santos officials demanded an extra 'upfront' payment of £2,500 (a considerable amount of money in those days) before allowing their team to play the game. Effectively, Plymouth Argyle were being held to ransom; and the club president of Santos was unrelenting in his demand. Reluctantly, the then Argyle Club chairman, Robert Daniel, agreed to the extra payment. I understand that Argyle reported the matter to the Football Association and that some years later Santos refunded the money to Argyle.

The game kicked off and Argyle were exceptionally good. They got amongst their illustrious opponents unsettling them and, before we knew it, Argyle were 3–0 up. Mike Dowling scored an absolute screamer, Derek Rickard with a glancing header made it two and Jimmy Hinch scored the third.

Anyone who was there that night should remember a number of cynical Santos fouls. Johnny Hore was to tell me years later that, using sign language, he and Pele agreed to tone the game down a little. Funnily enough, as a result of that, the second half belonged to Santos, who scored twice through Pele and, I think, Edu. All of the goals were scored at the Barn Park end.

After the game there were thousands of fans on the pitch, including me, celebrating a famous victory for the Greens. The attendance that night was just under 38,000 and remarkably over 20,000 came back the following Saturday to see us beat Bournemouth 1–0.

Fast forward forty years and I had the privilege of hosting the Santos forty-year reunion where ten of the side that played that night were present.

Johnny Hore revealed that he still has Pele's shirt (unsigned) and local referee Charlie Nicholls has the match ball. I am privileged to say that I eventually did get Pele's autograph on a match-day programme courtesy of my dear friend the late Graham Little.

We enquired about having Pele at the reunion. We were quoted a price of $1million.

Norman:

I went to the Santos game with my father. Now, I should say that I am about six feet tall whilst Dad was probably only just on the plus side of five feet and, as Paul has mentioned, the crowd on that day was close to 38,000. Unfortunately, there would not have been room to place my somewhat disgruntled father on a stool and I think he spent most of the game where we were in the Barn Park end moaning about how 'bloody ridiculous it was that he could not see' whilst I, on the other hand, was able to view the marvellous scene that unfolded before me.

It has since been suggested to me that maybe I was the milkman's son!

'No Introduction Needed'

Wednesday 23 January 1974

Plymouth Argyle v Manchester City
League Cup Semi-final, First Leg – 2.00 pm Kick Off
Paul:
This game sticks in my memory for a number of reasons. I was now into music as well and the number one hit record was 'Tiger Feet' by a group called Mud. This was very apt as the pitch was muddy and heavy. My Argyle were in the semi-finals of the League Cup for only the second time in their history and there was no way I was going to miss this game.

The problem was that because of power cuts, it was an afternoon kick off and the big boss of Tecalemit Garage Equipment, where I worked, had told everyone that nobody was to go to the game and that he had told the managing director of the whole Tecalemit Group that no one on his watch would be missing from work. Well, he didn't stand a chance and three of us, Roger Metcalfe, Dave Bogue and I, left for lunch that Wednesday and didn't come back. I can't remember the circumstances, but we had grandstand tickets just to the left of the halfway line. Apart from the odd reserve game, when you were allowed up at half time if it was cold, this was the first time I had been in the stand.

The view was brilliant, and we were right in Steve Davey's eye line when he scored with the outside of his right foot from the corner of the penalty area to put us 1–0 up. The 30,000-plus crowd erupted and all thoughts of 'Had we been missed at work?' disappeared in an instant.

Now City had some side. Their forward line was Summerbee, Bell, Lee, Law and the villain that was Rodney Marsh.

Villain because on Boxing Day 1967 he conned the referee to win a penalty which Mike Keen scored at the Devonport end to give QPR a 1–0 win. Yes, even now it still rankles. However, returning to the Man City game, it

68

was a centre half, Tommy Booth, who equalised with a header before half time. Once again, Argyle were excellent that afternoon, as they had been throughout that League Cup run, and fully deserved the 1–1 draw.

After the game and for the rest of the evening, my thoughts turned to work the next day; to be honest, I was sh…ing myself as we had been told severe consequences would await anyone who went to the game.

Morning arrived and sure enough we had been missed. I think we were summoned individually, and I know I was told I had let the boss down, the company down and myself down. The boss, Richard Cox (Dick), was so angry, I thought he was going to hit me. Oh, for Henry Menyena to be by my side!

The boss knew I was a massive Argyle fan and told me the day off I had booked for the second leg the following Wednesday was cancelled. Needless to say, I didn't go to Maine Road and it probably saved my job. Things were never quite the same after that and I left two years later.

Norman:

I too well remember the Manchester City game; unlike Harty, I was by now in the early stages of my career as a guardian of the law. Yes, can you believe that the boy from Camels Head – sorry, Swilly – was now a police officer?

I was posted to Exeter and had recently met the girl (and at that time she was little more than a girl) who would later become my wonderful wife, Deborah (Deb). Since Deb and I were in the early stages of our relationship, I had not managed to fully convert her to the green side of football; now, all these years later, we, along with our son, David, are all season ticket holders at the Theatre of Greens.

Thanks to shift work, I was able to attend the game with a colleague and, as Paul has mentioned, the game was played on a Wednesday afternoon; this was due to the fact that under the Conversative government (led by Prime Minister Ted

Heath) of the day, owing to industrial action by both coalminers and rail workers, the three-day week was one of several measures introduced in the UK in order to conserve electricity, therefore Argyle were not permitted to use their floodlights.

I still wonder if there was anyone working in the dockyard or, it would seem, at Tecalemit Garage with an attendance at Home Park in excess of 30,000 on a mid-week afternoon.

I think the three-day week on that occasion must have been somewhat truncated in Plymouth. One interesting fact about the game that day was that the referee who was originally to control the game, a Mr Reynolds, apparently injured his neck overnight and so the match started being refereed by the senior linesman before a Mr Yates, who had been called in as an emergency replacement, arrived from Worcestershire and took over about twenty-five minutes or so into the game.

I think some Manchester City players thought it was a bit of a 'sauce' that the new ref was allowed to come on and take over, particularly since he booked Mike Summerbee about three minutes or so after taking control.

Like Paul, I was very much into music and indeed I still am; I think my time as the choir claxon in the Devonport end set me up nicely and I later did join the Exeter Police Choir, where the highlight was participating at the first festival of Police Male Voice Choirs held at the Royal Albert Hall on Saturday 21 February 1987, with proceeds benefiting the Save the Children Fund. Fortunately, I didn't miss an Argyle home match on that day since they were away at Sheffield United and lost 2–1.

Similarly to Paul, I was unable to attend the second leg at Maine Road, but I was able to listen on the radio to the devastating 2–0 defeat when Colin Bell and Francis Lee were both on the score sheet for City.

Oh, what could have been!

Saturday 14 December 1974
Plymouth Argyle v Crystal Palace
FA Cup Second Round
Paul:
What a game this was! Over 17,000 at Home Park to see Argyle take on Crystal Palace, led by Malcolm Allison, our former manager. The Tony Waiters' revolution was gaining momentum, and Argyle came back from a goal down to win a tense game 2–1.

The two Argyle goals in the final twenty minutes were scored by Mike Green and Billy Rafferty. In stoppage time, the Devonport end went wild as Jim Furnell saved a penalty from Terry Venables.

It was a magical moment on a magical day. Jim Furnell said it was his most memorable moment in an Argyle shirt.

Anyone who was there must surely admit the tension was unbearable in a great game.

Abandonment for the Cause

Norman:

It's Saturday 11 January 1975. The conversion of my wife-to-be, Deb, is well underway. We, along with numerous members of the green ensemble from Devon, have made the trip to Bournemouth to support our heroes who are flying high in Division Three. The excitement is palpable; could this be the season?

So, the game began, and the Greens were 2–0 up within the first fifteen minutes or so. I became slightly distracted by my wonderful wife-to-be, who started to complain of feeling unwell. Now, Deb used to suffer with migraines, which I know can be very debilitating. I, on the other hand, at that moment was suffering, I think, from a severe bout of 'Argyleitus'. What to do? I could not let my partner be alone, so I escorted her to an area at the back of a stand, in order to attend to her needs. Unfortunately, the pitch could not be seen from that location but the roar of the Argyle fans as our team scored again was most certainly heard.

What a dilemma! How could I leave her? So, thinking on my Argyle feet, I glanced around and whilst my beloved was quite unwell, I spied an unsuspecting colleague from the local police force. I quickly explained my predicament and he, obviously like myself, being a keen, committed and understanding public servant, offered to supervise my poorly partner, whom I should say was clearly still supportive of the Argyle as I think she had turned herself a bright shade of green.

Who says I can't multitask? I clearly did my dual duty by supporting both loves of my life.

Incidentally we went on to win 7–3 and won promotion in second place behind Blackburn Rovers, whom we beat on the evening of Tuesday 4 February 1975 at Home Park in front of over 28,000 fans; Charlton Athletic finished third in the league that season. We actually drew with them at

Home Park on the Saturday after the Blackburn game in front of nearly 23,000. The score that day was 1–1 and I'm sorry to remind Billy Rafferty that he missed a penalty in the last minute of the Charlton game, having earlier put us 1–0 up. Sorry, Billy.

Oh, by the way, Deb recovered from her period of malaise at the Bournemouth match and, all these years later, I think she has just about forgiven me for the abandonment.

I wonder if visiting Bournemouth was part of my inspiration for later becoming part of the police family, because I can also remember being at Bournemouth in August of 1968 for an evening kick off when Argyle won 1–0 with the goal being scored by Dave Burnside. When he scored, I was so overcome with emotion that I ran and hugged one of the nearest people to me; it so happened that this person was a man wearing a dark blue uniform and sporting a rather grand piece of headgear. Yes, you are right, I hugged a police officer; fortunately, he seemed reasonably comfortable with my act of passion and I was able to watch the lads win the game.

Now, when I became an officer of the law, I would almost certainly have allowed a similar act of exuberance (well, maybe not in the Cowshed Stand at the ground of Exeter City).

Just the Ticket
Norman:

Clearly with my then fiancée almost completely converted a) to football and more importantly b) to the Greens, it was with much expectation and no little excitement that I looked forward to taking her to Home Park to watch my heroes play against Everton in the fourth round of the FA Cup.

The game was due to be played on Saturday 25 January 1975, just a couple of weeks after the 7–3 drubbing of Bournemouth. The game against Everton (then managed by the great Billy Bingham) was going to be a sell-out and tickets were obviously at a premium. Mindful of the fact that many Argyle fans would be at the Bournemouth away game, it was arranged that fans who had attended that match with proof of attendance would be able to purchase a ticket for the all-important clash with the 'Toffees' (the nickname of Everton).

Not a problem for me and my beloved then! Ahh, but we did not live in Plymouth. Enter my marvellous second mum, Mrs H; she would be able to get the tickets, but alas she arrived at Home Park to be informed there were no more – *no mâs* (my Janner translation to Spanish) – tickets available.

Devastated is probably an understatement of my predicament at that time. I have to confess that Argyle have brought me to the brink of tears on more than one occasion and this would have been almost certainly a meltdown situation.

I was so upset that I felt it only right that I expressed my extreme disappointment that I would be excluded from such an important match and so a letter was sent possibly in desperation rather than hope to the home of the Greens.

The stars must have been aligned for me at that time as I received a wonderful reply with two tickets for which I gratefully paid the cost of, as I recall, £1.00 (50p each) and

I was able to go with my wife-to-be to watch the game. Yes, it ended in a 3–1 defeat in front of about 38,000 fans, however just to be there, as I feel sure all football fans will understand, was almost my raison d'étre (I don't just do Spanish!) as an Argyle fan.

Tuesday 15 April 1975
Plymouth Argyle v Colchester United
Division Three – Evening Kick Off
Paul:

I attended this game with my brother Phil, who was down from Durham University for this match and for what turned out to be the infamous game at Peterborough.

My first promotion, and what an emotional night. After almost fifteen years of following the Super Greens, I finally knew what it was like to be promoted. We were one of the first into the ground to make sure we secured our place behind my usual crush barrier in the Lower Mayflower Stand.

There was an air of expectation that night. We were a good side, and Colchester were mid-table; surely this was it? Roared on by over 23,000 fans, Argyle made a dominant start, but a combination of good goalkeeping and last-ditch defending meant it was goalless at the interval.

Undeterred, the fans were brilliant and early in the second half, Argyle scored. Inevitably, the fantastic duo of Paul Mariner and Billy Rafferty were involved; when Billy squared the ball across the six-yard box, Paul was first to react and slammed the ball home, the only goal of the game.

Our view from the Barn Park end of the Lower Mayflower stand could not have been better. Colchester were not there just to make up the numbers and made it a very nervy last twenty minutes before the ref finally blew for full time.

Fans had been gathering around the perimeter of the pitch and the atmosphere was manic, but brilliant, as everyone it seemed was on the pitch and a lot of the players were carried off shoulder high. It was ages before the pitch was cleared, but nobody cared. The Greens were going up.

The celebrations were long and loud, and it was nearly 9.45 pm before the players left the pitch.

The journey home to Mount Gould Road (we had moved there from Penlee Place) was only interrupted by a couple of celebratory beers in the Mutley Tavern.

Little did I know then there would be more drama between Argyle and Colchester some twenty-one years later.

The next game was on Saturday 19 April at Home Park against Port Vale, when Argyle, having secured promotion, were applauded onto the pitch by Port Vale players prior to the start of the match. The game played in front of a crowd in excess of 22,000 ended in a 1–1 draw. Unfortunately, Colin Randell was sent off – but still, Argyle had already been promoted.

Saturday 26 April 1975

Peterborough United v Plymouth Argyle
Division Three – 3.00 pm Kick Off
Paul:

For what turned out to be an infamous game I was able to secure two tickets. It was the final game of that season for Argyle. I am not sure but I think I obtained the tickets through my local football connections. Travel to and from the game was provided on a private hire coach, which was to leave from outside a local pub on Embankment Road, Plymouth.

The pub, which has long since closed, was called the Black Prince and was certainly not an establishment that Phil and I would normally frequent, as I don't believe it would have gained a Michelin star for its welcoming qualities to non-locals.

So it was that on the Friday evening before the game at Peterborough, Cambridgeshire, my younger sibling and I walked from my mother's house in Mount Gould Road, Plymouth, to the aforementioned public house. Public houses then normally closed at 10.30 pm but on Fridays they were allowed an extension to 11.00 pm and so the coach was due to leave at 11.30 pm.

Phil and I arrived in good time and realised that we hardly knew any of our fellow travellers, but we were going to the game and had high expectations of an Argyle victory and, as far as I was concerned, this mode of transport was far better than hitchhiking.

During the first two hours or so of our journey there were numerous 'comfort' stops as many of the clientele on the coach found it necessary to dispense with much of the excess alcohol they had consumed earlier in the evening. The coach passengers then largely settled into deep slumber. I cannot recall if there was mass snoring or not!

We arrived in Peterborough at about 7 am on the day of the game.

As the morning went on, I would estimate about 6,000 Argyle fans had arrived in the city of Peterborough; unfortunately, there were sporadic pockets of trouble throughout the time leading up to the 3.00 pm kick off, trouble which fortunately my brother and I avoided.

We arrived at the London Road ground of Peterborough (which is now named the Weston Homes Stadium) and purchased a programme which cost 10p; our entrance tickets cost 65p each and were for a terrace on one side of the pitch.

There was a crowd in excess of 11,000, with the majority of the Argyle fans being housed behind one of the goals.

Argyle went behind in the forty-second minute with the game ending 1–0 to the home team; sadly, at the final whistle a hundred or so 'Greens' fans entered the field of play and I recall two police officers forlornly trying to detain an Argyle fan; however, these officers were outnumbered. Meanwhile, the hundred or so Plymouth fans had entered the away end and although they became involved in a very serious confrontation with opposition supporters, they soon began to be overrun. This seemed to be the catalyst for a mass exodus of virtually all of the remaining Plymouth supporters behind the goal. From my position of relative safety in an area to one side of the pitch, I saw that a frightening and potentially very dangerous situation was probably averted when the Peterborough fans quickly dispersed. I have never seen home supporters disappear as fast as they did that day.

Phil and I returned to our coach and very soon were on our way back to Plymouth. When we arrived home, our mother asked how our day had been. We informed her that it was just your normal average away game!

Football hooliganism at that time was prevalent and it gives me no pleasure to relate an experience of a game involving my beloved Plymouth Argyle where the headlines of the day were about the disturbing behaviour of some of our fans rather than what had occurred during the game itself.

Blackburn Rovers went on to become champions of Division Three that season, with Argyle promoted in second place along with third-placed Charlton Athletic.

Saturday 6 September 1975

Plymouth Argyle v Sunderland
Division Two – 3.00 pm Kick Off
Paul:
Having returned to the second division after a seven-year absence, the big question was: could we stay there?

A huge test early in the season was Sunderland at home. The visitors were favourites to win the league and had won the FA Cup only eighteen months previously. One of the heroes of that day in 1973, when second division Sunderland beat Leeds United 1–0 to lift the famous trophy, was one Micky Horswill. Micky was by now an Argyle player, having signed for the Greens from Manchester City in the summer of 1975.

I went to the game with my brother, Phil, and for some reason we stood on the Mayflower terracing, to the right of the dug outs. We had a great view from there and I remember saying: 'If we get something out of this game, we will be OK.'

There was a big crowd and a large away following; the atmosphere was great even without a roof over our heads.

Argyle attacked the Devonport end in the first half and played really well. Sunderland, being a good side, had their moments but it remained 0–0 at half time.

Then it happened!

Two minutes into the second half, Billy Rafferty received the ball just inside the touch line where we were standing. He went on a magical run and with the Sunderland defence backing off, he cut inside on his left foot and fired into the bottom corner of the net from the edge of the penalty area. I remember that goal as if it was yesterday. It was a great game, settled by a great goal, scored by a great player. And, yes, I was right; we stayed up that season.

Later that night, or should I say the early hours of Sunday morning, we celebrated in Chantelle's Night Club with John Delve and Micky Horswill. Sunderland did go up as champions.

Sacrifice

Saturday 22 November 1975 – the boy from Swilly was marrying Deb. Her full conversion to becoming a Green was almost complete.

12 noon – the hour for the ceremony at Lympstone Church to take place.

I love my wife dearly, but perhaps naively I had clearly not checked the fixtures for that particular day: West Bromwich Albion at Home Park. I would have to miss it; still, the only consolation was that guess who was our best man? Well, if I was going to miss it, Paul would have to as well.

I think the two of us cut a mighty dash in our morning suits whilst carrying top hats (reminds me that I once had a cardboard Argyle top hat).

My bride was stunning in her wonderful white dress and, yes, I did resist any temptation to paint green stripes on it to align with an Argyle shirt.

The ceremony went superbly well and we are still very happily married. I am pleased to report that full conversion to green status was bestowed upon my darling wife many years ago and she has become a regular in the Lyndhurst Stand and has held a season ticket for several years.

The reception was held at her parents' wonderful house in Lympstone, Devon, overlooking the Exe Estuary. We left in our Vauxhall Viva motor car, complete with kippers on the engine block, and trailing various cans and the like behind us.

I, of course, could not forsake the Pilgrims and had to check the result on the car radio. I am extremely pleased to say there were two winners that day: me and, of course, the victorious Greens, who won 2–1.

How lucky was I!

Norman and Paul
Saturday 22 November 1975 – Lympstone Church, Devon
"I reckon they will win 2–1 today"

Norman and Deb – Saturday 22 November 1975
Norman wondering if he still has time to get to
Home Park for the match!

Best Behaviour

Norman:

In 1977, as a result of violence at the first round, first leg European Cup Winners' cup tie between Saint Etienne and Manchester United in France, when the match ended in a 1–1 draw, United were subsequently banned from the competition; however, on appeal, they were reinstated provided they paid a fine and agreed to play the second leg tie at least 200 kilometres from Old Trafford, Manchester. No tickets were to be sold in Manchester for this second game and lots of locations were considered but dismissed.

Enter little old Third Division Plymouth Argyle, whose chairman of the day, Robert Daniel, clearly after positive canvassing, was able to get Home Park selected as the venue for the game. Since tickets could not be sold in Manchester for this match, the enterprising Home Park hierarchy made 10,000 vouchers available at Argyle's home game against Gillingham, with each voucher allowing the purchase of two tickets for the Manchester United game which finally took place on Wednesday 5 October 1977 at Home Park, with an attendance in excess of 31,500. Apparently, there was also a big screen at Old Trafford where around 38,000 fans watched the game.

Now, this game was clearly a high-profile event in view of what had happened in the first leg and so it was that about a hundred officers were drafted in to police the match from around the Devon and Cornwall Police Force; I was one of them. I well remember that around the running track surrounding the pitch, officers were strategically placed in twos on chairs, with one officer facing the fans to ensure that there were no crowd incidents and the other officer facing the pitch to ensure the safety of their colleague, for how embarrassing and possibly painful would it have been if a thirty-yard screamer from Lou Macari or Jimmy

Greenhoff had connected with the top knot of one of the unsuspecting members of the local constabulary?

Both my partner on the day and I were stationed at the Barn Park end and were keen football fans, so both of us wanted to face the pitch. Compromise was reached and we agreed that we would swap places at fifteen-minute intervals with the pitch-facer commentating on the game to his partner. I am pleased to say that I was facing the pitch for both of the United goals in a 2–0 victory for the Red Devils, (the nickname of Manchester United). They went out of the competition in the next round, losing to Porto.

The game went off without any major incidents; there were no arrests, I like to think because of good policing but also that us Janners are a well-behaved lot.

Once a Green, Always a Green

Norman:

As a police officer in Exeter, I often found myself working at Exeter City home games and so it was no surprise that on New Year's Day, 1980, I found myself a part of the match-day policing team in what was then the main standing area, known as the Cowshed, where the main Exeter choir assembled. I was helping to oversee the police operation, whilst their team took on the mighty side from down the A38.

There was a crowd of more than 10,000 in the ground, and clearly in view of the local derby status of the game and the love and affection each set of supporters have for one another, I am sure there was peace and tranquillity all around – NOT.

I was in full uniform, calmly and professionally going about my allocated task. Argyle went 2–0 down and as I'm sure was the case for the many Argyle fans in the ground, my heart sank. Of course, I remained outwardly calm and certainly attentive to the job in hand – then Colin Randell pulled one back; Colin initially came to Argyle in 1973 before signing for Exeter in 1977, but then returning to Argyle from the dark side in 1979 to play once again for the Super Greens.

I felt a tingle of quiet excitement that Argyle were back in the game and there would have been, I'm sure, some concern amongst the Cowshed faithful. Of course, I continued, outwardly anyway, to remain my ever calm and professional self.

Then it happened! I still have a memory of that man, Colin Randell, careering down the left side of the St James's Park pitch and planting a superb equaliser into the City net at the end of the ground that housed the majority of Argyle fans.

At that point, I must confess, all of my internal emotions exploded into a crescendo of excitement and in amongst the disillusioned Cowshed, filled with Exeter fans, was one uniformed police officer jumping up and down, displaying unbridled passion and exuberance.

I'm sorry, Exeter fans; I'm sure you understand, but what was an ardent Green supposed to do, the lone voice in a red wilderness?

Wednesday 14 March 1984

Derby County v Plymouth Argyle

FA Cup Sixth Round Replay– 7.30 pm Kick Off

Paul:

This was a truly memorable night as Argyle progressed through to the semi-final of the FA Cup.

I went to this game with Phil, and we decided to do it in style. We had queued for tickets at Home Park when they went on sale on the Sunday morning and we both went into our places of work on the Monday to say we were taking the Wednesday and Thursday off.

We travelled to Derby by National Express and stayed overnight in a city hotel. The coach fare was £17.00 return to Derby.

With Argyle being the better side in the first game at Home Park in front of a crowd of just over 34,000, when they drew 0–0, we travelled more in hope than anything else; after all, they had Kenny Burns, Archie Gemmill, Bobby Davidson, Dave Watson, John Robertson and a certain Steve Cherry (Steve was later to become a goalkeeper with the Greens) on their side. However, the closer we got to Derby, the more we began to think: We can do this. There were not that many people on the coach and so we could spread out and relax and by the time we arrived, we were pretty confident.

A quick check into our hotel (The Midland) and it was off to the ground. There were thousands of Argyle fans there, most packed behind the goal, and hundreds, including us, in the grandstand.

The atmosphere in and around the ground was hostile, on a par with Leeds, eleven years earlier, but when there are hundreds of you all together, it seems less intimidating.

'Every man jack' of that Argyle side were amazing that night, one of the best team performances I have ever seen. Derby started on the front foot, as you would expect, but didn't create any clear-cut chances. Argyle looked dangerous and in one of their breaks they won a corner on the left. Andy Rogers trotted over to take it and the rest is history. A pure fluke, he would later describe it as, his corner beating Steve Cherry at his near post and sailing high into the net. The scenes behind the goal were incredible, matched by the Argyle faithful in the grandstand. I hugged and kissed two girls sat next to us (any excuse) as the whole place went wild. Little did I know then that I would become good friends with one of the girls, Barbara, for years to come.

It was 1–0 to the Argyle and 'We shall not be moved' rang out across the Baseball Ground (the then home stadium of Derby County). Incredibly, Lindsay Smith could have made it two before half time, his shot crashing against the bar. Into the second half Derby were getting more and more anxious, and Argyle were playing brilliantly and saw the game out to make it through to the semi-finals.

At the final whistle, all hell broke out. Missiles and objects rained down on the fans behind the goal and Derby fans in the stand tried to attack us; there were police and stewards everywhere. Outside the ground it was frightening with fights breaking out all over the place. The scarves were hidden as we thought about finding our way back to the hotel. There were Derby fans wherever we looked trying to get us to speak by saying: 'Are you from Plymouth?' or 'Have you got a light, mate?' The police were used to handling big games and we made it back to the hotel in one piece.

The hotel bar was packed, and the drinks flowed. We had a meal in the bar and watched the highlights on *Match of the Day*. It was a great end to a great night. We were later to hear that the Argyle team had also stayed in the hotel.

Apparently, Kevin Hodges ended up carrying Chris Harrison to his room. Chris has since told me that this was the only time in his life he can recall being drunk.

The following morning it was time for a leisurely breakfast whilst reading the papers. The front pages were dominated by the miners' strike whilst the back pages were all about the Super Greens great win.

A night and performance I will never forget.

A Miner Problem

Norman:

Alas, Paul's visit to Derby when the Argyle won their place in the semi-final of the FA Cup (of which more from yours truly later) was not a match I attended.

At that time, the miners' strike had only recently commenced and I became a part of the Devon and Cornwall Constabulary police contingent making regular pilgrimages (if you will forgive the pun), mostly to Derbyshire, to support the local forces in the policing of a dispute which went on for approximately one year.

When we went to help police in the long-running dispute, we were usually away for the best part of a week at a time.

I guess the distance to Villa Park, Birmingham, the neutral ground where the game was to be played, from where I was billeted during the week leading up to that 'never-to-be-forgotten' semi-final encounter with Watford, was about fifty miles or so. Sometimes our police units would be released on Fridays to return home and sometimes it could be, as I recall, on a Saturday. How could a committed green-blooded person not attend an historic day as was about to unfold on Saturday 14 April 1984?

Not knowing whether we could leave Derbyshire on the Friday or the Saturday, it was clearly imperative that arrangements be made, yes, to reassociate myself with my darling wife and by then two daughters, Sarah and Rebecca (our son Dave at that time had not appeared on the scene for his indoctrination as a member of the Green Army) but, of course, there is a hierarchy of needs to consider as I am sure you will understand. So obviously, arrangements were put in place that I would either be dropped off in Birmingham, if we left Derbyshire on the Saturday of the game, and a neighbour from Exeter would drive some 160 miles or more to meet me in order to attend the game, or if we returned on the Friday, then I would be available to travel to Birmingham.

In the event, the latter of the above options ensued and so I was able to perform my family duties, I accept albeit for a relatively short period of time, and, of course, my duty to the Super Greens. I recall the irony of being searched as a matter of routine on entering Villa Park, an irony which was not lost on me bearing in mind the duties I had been performing in the preceding days.

One thing that my family still often hear me say when that glorious, if disappointing, 1–0 semi-final loss, at least amongst us Greens, is mentioned is: 'John Barnes down the left, crosses the ball, big George Riley, boom, one nil, end of game'. How close did we come to glory on that day?

Saturday 2 March 1985
Plymouth Argyle v Doncaster Rovers
Division Three – 3.00 pm Kick Off
Paul:
If ever the chant 'You dirty Northern Bast….' was apt, it was for Doncaster Rovers that day.

It was not a great season; we finished fifteenth, but Dave Smith had been appointed manager in November 1984 and his enthusiasm was starting to have an impact.

The faithful 5,000 were there that day and I was on the Mayflower Terrace quite close to the away dug out, able to hear every word.

The main villains were the Snodin brothers, Glyn and Ian, who literally kicked and gave verbals to everyone who came near them. The few fans, including me, were becoming more incensed by the minute and when Doncaster took the lead, things threatened to boil over, but Argyle were not to be denied that day and Kevin Summerfield equalised. Both the Snodin brothers were given terrible abuse and Ian in particular lost it. When 'Sir' Tommy Tynan (as he is affectionally known by many Argyle fans) scored a late winner, the Argyle fans really laid into Ian, so much so he said he would see us outside afterwards.

He was true to his word and only a combination of their officials and Argyle stewards prevented a tense situation becoming ugly. People who know me are aware that I am the most placid guy going, but I swear to God I could have punched him that day. Anyone else recall this game?

Promoting the Greens

Norman:

Having finished fourth in the old Division Three in the 1995/96 season, Plymouth Argyle found themselves in the 'play-offs' for promotion to Division Two. Colchester had finished in seventh position with Darlington fifth and Hereford sixth.

So it was that Argyle played Colchester at their home ground, Layer Road, on Sunday 12 May 1996 in the first leg of the Division Three play-off semi-final. The match ended in a 1–0 victory for Colchester.

Three days later, on Wednesday 15 May, the second leg took place at Home Park, in front of a crowd of about 14,500; I remember the atmosphere was electric and was raised even further when, after approximately three minutes, Mickey Evans scored to put the teams' level on aggregate. Just before half time, Chris Leadbitter scored for Argyle to set the home fans dreaming of a final on the hallowed Wembley turf.

Colchester clearly had other ideas and in the sixty-sixth minute, Kinsella scored for them to restore parity; drama abounded as Argyle manager, the great Neil Warnock, was sent off for protesting after Adrian Littlejohn was brought down by Tony McCarthy of Colchester when Littlejohn was 'in-on-goal'; Neil Warnock and many of the crowd were incensed when only a yellow card was shown to the Colchester man.

Neil Warnock then climbed into the crowd in the Mayflower Stand from where he was able to shout instructions; who says there is no passion in sport?

With the game level on aggregate, Paul Williams (lovingly nicknamed Charlie Williams after a well-known comedian of the day), having got himself into the Colchester penalty area from his left-back position, threw himself at a Martin Barlow cross from the right and scored with a header past the Colchester keeper. At the final whistle the crowd went wild – the Greens were going to Wembley.

The rest, as they say, is history. On Saturday 25 May, about 30,000 Argyle fans, in a crowd of over 43,000, witnessed the Argyle Legend that is Ronnie Mauge score the only goal of the game as the men from Home Park beat Darlington to clinch promotion to Division Two.

Paul:

I was fortunate enough to attend both legs of the fiercely contested semi-final. We were totally outplayed in the first leg and only the heroics of goalkeeper Steve Cherry, making his 100th appearance, kept the score at 1–0 to Colchester. The mood on the supporters' coach on the long drive home was surprisingly buoyant. After all, in a two-legged tie, to come away from home and only lose 1–0 was deemed in those days a positive result.

I watched the return leg from the Lyndhurst Stand with my daughter Rachel. It was one of those nights that will live long in the memory, not only for the result but the fact I had a quality evening with my daughter. Little did I know that night that I would later hold two Wembley reunions: twenty- and twenty-five-year anniversary events.

The first event was in March 2016 when twelve players made an emotional return to Home Park for the game versus Luton Town. The players had a wonderful day, climaxed by a dinner at the Duke of Cornwall Hotel, Plymouth. Undoubtedly, the highlight of a great evening was the arrival of Neil Warnock at around 10 pm. He had driven 320 miles from Norwich where his then team, Rotherham United, had played that day.

I remember vividly the buzz in the room, which was already electric, when Neil walked in. After he had been embraced by his former players and fans, I had the privilege of interviewing him. It was only afterwards when Neil found time for a sandwich that he was later heard to say: 'I would not have missed this for the world.'

The second event was on Friday 9 October 2021 in Club Argyle. This was another fantastic event co-hosted by me and the late great 'Sir Gordon Sparks', as he is known to this day by many Argyle fans. The following day the team were guests of Plymouth Argyle for their home game against Burton Albion. Twenty-five years on, there is still a tremendous bond between the players and the 'gaffer' Neil Warnock. I have found that in all our successful sides, the bond between players and management remains to this day.

We're Not Talking Anymore

Norman:

It's August 1996, summer is slowly evaporating into its final throws and the new football season is just a few games in. Argyle have had a very satisfactory start and after four league games in Division Two, they are top.

My family and I were staying with friends in Northumberland and, as far as I was aware, the Greens were due to play Preston North End at Home Park on Saturday 31 August. No problem! We would make the long journey back to our home in Exeter on the Friday; my darling wife has a relative in Macclesfield, Cheshire, and so we could break the journey back to Devon, visiting the relative before travelling home to arrive on Friday evening ready for the short hop to Home Park the next day. Perfect, don't you think?...

Well, not quite – there's a saying from 'To a Mouse' by Robert Burns – 'The best laid schemes o' mice an' men gang aft a gley,' meaning that basically your best-laid plans can go awry.

I doubt that Robert Burns was an Argyle fan, but how apt those words were on that occasion.

On that fateful Friday, as we were preparing to leave our friends in Northumberland, I believe it was Deb who discovered that the live match which was originally due to be televised on the Friday evening had earlier been postponed and in its place the Argyle versus Preston game was to be moved back from the Saturday to the Friday evening: 'Oh no, Deb, you should have realised sooner we cannot stay in Northumberland. We have to go via Macclesfield and we won't be able to watch the game there. This is a disaster and it cannot be my fault.'

Off we set in total silence, no one daring to speak to me, and I certainly was not in the mood for conversation whilst contemplating the circumstances which had befallen me.

The 'coup de grâce' and possibly the only grunt that could be heard by me was that en route to Macclesfield we passed road signs for Preston, whence I was probably heard to mumble – 'Bloody marvellous, Preston's only a few miles away but we are playing in Plymouth.' I had wanted to postpone our visit to Macclesfield in the forlorn hope that we might still reach Plymouth in time for the evening game, but Deb was having none of it and she insisted that we continued to see her relative as no doubt tea and cake would almost certainly have been laid on as well as there being, I am sure, very interesting (and lengthy) family catch-up chat, not much of it centring on the Argyle.

I must confess, Deb's relatives were lovely and I did mellow somewhat, making the journey from Macclesfield to Exeter far less tense. I should say that the positive from the experience was that Argyle did win 2–1, with Mickey Evans and Richard Logan scoring for the Greens. I did eventually speak again to my darling wife and even though I know I would have apologised a long time ago, I now wish to show deep contrition to her and apologise yet again.

Oh, the traumas of being an Argyle fan.

Simply Amazing

Norman:

It's wonderful how football can unite and even though we Greens look at others whom we consider less fortunate than ourselves to support teams that sport different colours (for example red and white) and maybe are based 'up the road' from the Theatre of Greens, nevertheless for true supporters and, I am sure, for many players, the language of football is one of unity and friendship.

Many years ago, whilst serving as a police officer, I one day had to visit someone who lived on 'my patch' in Exeter in order to arrange the renewal of his shotgun certificate. As it turned out, this affable young man was a professional footballer; well, he played for 'you know who' at the time.

In all seriousness, he was a nice guy who hailed from Ormskirk, just a few miles north of Liverpool. I remember he challenged me to a game of badminton, which I politely and, I think, somewhat sensibly declined. Although I felt I was quite reasonable at the game, there were, as I saw it, two obstacles in the way: one, he was many years younger than me; and two, he was a very fit professional sportsman. I think if he ran me so ragged that afterwards I would struggle to put one knee in front of the other - for I fear I would have found it difficult to use my feet for some time after the proposed encounter - apart from not being able to walk properly for some time, the ignominy of an Argle fan being brought to his knees by an Exeter City player may have been too much to bear.

Fast forward to 2023, Deb and I are guests at the Argyle versus Swansea match at the Theatre of Greens, courtesy of a very kind gentleman who was a season ticket holder at Home Park, but who was not in the best of health. We used to transport him to Argyle games from Exeter and he wanted to say thank you to us, a very generous and kind (if not necessary) gesture for which Deb and I were very grateful.

Paul was the compere at the event and during it, he mentioned that there was somebody there who used to play for (can I say it?) Exeter City – there, I've done it. It was one John Hodge. 'I know John Hodge,' I tell Deb, who then orders – sorry, suggests – that I speak to him. I seek John out and I recount the story of the police officer who renewed his shotgun certificate all those years ago; John remembers and I say, "I was that policeman."

John played sixty-five times for the team from up the road and then for Swansea 102 times, moving on to Walsall, Gillingham and Northampton.

On Saturday 10 April 1993 – now, fellow Greens' fans, this may hurt – he scored twice at the Barn Park end for Exeter in a 3–0 victory over Argyle, but in the spirit of harmony and a newfound friendship with John, I do not hold it against him, even though his head over heels 'somersault' in front of the jubilant City fans probably felt like a dagger to the hearts of despondent Argyle supporters; however, I still have no intention of playing badminton with him.

Simply amazing – well done, John – Top Man.

Living the Dream – Football Manager

Paul:

I had often wondered what it might be like to manage a football team. To manage a team of ex-professional Plymouth Argyle players never even entered my head and although it sounds ridiculous, that is eventually what happened when I became the manager of the Argyle Legends. I have come to the conclusion that as far as playing games goes, footballers like to be managed. Therefore, we have a match-day structure which gives the players a time of arrival when they are issued with warm-up tops to prepare with, along with plenty of heat rub, together with the system we are going to play. The players' shorts are hung up in the changing room prior to them arriving in order to make it as professional as possible.

As the changing room fills up, the banter commences and is priceless – it continues right up to the time of kick off. Make no mistake, these guys want to win; that competitive edge and winning mentality drilled into them as young men never leaves them.

The mind is ready, the desire is there, although on occasions the body lets them down, especially when playing against opponents thirty years (yes, I mean thirty years!) younger.

I have lost count of the number of times it looked as if we were going to be beaten but, somehow, we have managed to 'nick a draw' or have snatched victory from the jaws of defeat.

I have nothing but respect for every one of them who continually give their Sundays in order to raise thousands of pounds for charities. They quite rightly refer to themselves as former players giving something back to the game.

I am proud of every player who wears the 'shirt', and to think they call me 'Gaffer' is to me, a humble Argyle fan, a dream come true. I'm living the dream.

Paul with his Legendary Band of Brothers

'LEGEND'

Paul:

One of the main objectives of the former players' association is its determination to make a difference to people's lives in the Southwest. This story, which I am proud to relate, endorses that mantra.

In November 2018, several members of the Argyle Legends attended a successful charity function at Boringdon Park Golf Club, Plymouth, one of whom was former Argyle Captain Leigh Cooper (Coops).

At subsequent Legends' charity events, Coops kept on saying that we (Argyle Legends) should undertake a major fundraising event. His persistence finally paid off when at Lanreath in Cornwall on Sunday 28 April 2019 during a wet and windy afternoon, the Legends' players bought into his idea.

Coops' vision was to raise £10,000 for The Guide Dogs for the Blind Association. With this sum we could put a guide dog pup through training, secure naming rights, have a couple of visits during the pup's training and change someone's life forever.

The seed was definitely sown and the Guide Dogs' Association were thrilled at the idea; it was agreed that the pup would be called LEGEND.

Preparations began immediately for the first event, a glittering charity ball at Boringdon Park. On Saturday 2 November 2019, 180 people, including many former Argyle players, enjoyed a sumptuous four-course meal which was followed by an auction and raffle. The evening was a tremendous success and the fantastic sum of £4,696 was raised.

The second initiative on Saturday 14 December was a bucket collection during half time at Argyle's home game against Morecambe. Thanks to the generosity of the fantastic Green Army, a further £1,445 was raised. A Just

Giving page, a donation from Mundial Studios and a bucket collection at the Avon Inn, South Brent, not far from Plymouth, raised a further £630.

We were well on the way, having reached two-thirds of our target in a matter of months. Then the pandemic arrived and to everyone's frustration, everything stopped. Move on twelve months to March 2021 and a subtle plan was hatched. Argyle Legends have over three hundred players in their Association; the idea was that if everyone contributed £10, we would almost hit our target. An email was sent explaining what we had set out to do, how far we had come and almost an apology asking for a £10 donation. The response was overwhelming. Donations came flooding in and within weeks, a further £1,670 was raised.

Then came the magical phone call that was to smash our target. I was sat at home on a Sunday evening when my phone rang; the name on the display was Neil Warnock. After dropping the phone in my excitement, I finally answered. The conversation was brief and typical of Neil. 'How much do you need?' he asked. 'I presume you are talking guide dogs?' I replied. Neil answered: 'Of course I am. How much do you need?' I said: 'We are still a couple of thousand short.' 'Leave it with me,' said Neil and put the phone down. That was it – end of the call.

About ten minutes later, there was a ping on my phone and a message saying, 'Two thousand pounds had been paid into the Legends' bank account.' I couldn't believe what I was reading. I immediately phoned him back and his lovely wife, Sharon, answered. I said that I had received an electronic message and just wanted to check that they hadn't entered an extra zero by mistake; after all, there is a huge difference between two hundred pounds and two thousand pounds. Sharon confirmed there was no error and, for once in my life, I was left speechless.

The Argyle Legends' family had come up trumps once again. The Guide Dogs' Association were naturally delighted to hear the news and plans were made for an official cheque presentation, which eventually took place at Home Park in June 2021.

LEGEND the pup subsequently went through an intensive eighteen-month training regime and is now a fully-fledged guide dog.

I am delighted to say that LEGEND was matched with a lady in South Devon and became her companion from March 2023. It is hoped that maybe one day LEGEND and his owner will visit Home Park, but this is dependent on his owner being agreeable to this; if she declines, sadly we will not see LEGEND again.

Naturally Argyle Legends are very proud of their achievement and on their behalf, I would like to express sincere thanks to everyone who contributed to this fantastic cause, which I am sure will be a real-life changer for the dog's new owner.

Take a bow-wow, you four-legged LEGEND.

Paul being introduced to 'LEGEND'
At Home Park

Paul with Neil Warnock at Tavistock, Devon

The Legend that is Forever Green

Paul:

After seventeen years of being known as Argyle Legends and following lengthy discussions with the football club, a new name for the Legends, 'Forever Green', was born.

On Saturday 20 January 2024, Forever Green was launched in front of a packed hospitality crowd in Club Argyle at the game versus Cardiff City. It had already been agreed that every player who had played first-team football would qualify for Forever Green status and would receive a presentation box containing a Forever Green scarf and a unique numbered pin badge. What an exciting challenge that would be, tracing families of players who had played since 1903. *That will keep me busy, as the new Forever Green ambassador*, I thought. Under this new idea, players, voted for by the Green Army, would receive icon status and be presented with a special award. The first five icons voted for and announced at the launch were:

Jack Leslie
Mike Bickle
Tommy Tynan
David Friio
Gary Sawyer.

At a subsequent event, Johnny Hore was also to receive icon status.

I am absolutely delighted to be involved. This transition into the football club will mean former players will continue to be remembered long after I have departed this world.

Prior to the transition, I had been heavily involved in establishing Argyle Legends into becoming one of the biggest former player associations in the UK. It wasn't always like that, I remember.

Back in 2004, Plymouth Argyle asked three fans, Andy Riddle, Tom Finnie and yours truly, if we could get 100 former players to attend the home game versus Wrexham to celebrate the centenary year of Plymouth Argyle. As a result of this, ninety players were paraded around the Home Park pitch prior to the game.

The following year, a private dinner was organised for the 1958/59 championship winning team at the Astor Hotel in Plymouth.

During this time, former players were being traced, and indeed some managers, and in 2007, following discussions with the then chief executive Michael Dunford, Argyle Legends was officially launched. The president of Argyle Legends was former player and manager John Hore with another ex-player, Steve Davey, being chairman and me secretary.

The constitution was:

1   To bring together former players and managers who had not seen each other for many years. This was mainly achieved through playing football matches, reunions, golf days and the popular match-day guest experiences.

2   To support local charities by organising a variety of events featuring the Legends team, alongside a cricket and skittles team. Money has been raised for charities such as St Luke's Hospice, Prostrate Cancer, Teenage Cancer Trust, Help Elsa Walk, Dame Hannah Rogers, Cancer Research and Orphaned Children, to name but a few. Currently a sum in excess of £107,000 has been raised.

3   To arrange for a Legend to be present at the opening of a shop or business.

4   To give children the opportunity to meet, in person, former players/managers their families have historically talked about.

5   To acknowledge those players and managers who have dazzled, mesmerised or even frustrated fans in the past and bring them into the Argyle Legends family. At the time of writing this book, former players and managers total 356 and include household names such as:

Billy Rafferty
Tommy Tynan
Peter Shilton
Jim Furnell
Norman Piper
Neil Warnock
Graham Coughlan
Kevin Hodges
Bruce Grobbelaar
Paul Sturrock
Taribo West
Romain Larrieu
David Friio
Johnny Hore
Mickey Heathcote
Paul Wotton.

Special Friends

Paul:

Over the years, I have had the privilege of meeting so many footballers, journalists and members of the media; the list could go on forever and whilst writing this chapter, I apologise to anyone whom I may not mention.

I constantly pinch myself when I think that some of the former players who I used to idolise are now good friends of mine.

I have already talked about **Mike Bickle** and his partner in a previous chapter and so, in no particular order, let's start with Argyle royalty, **Billy and Elaine Rafferty** – the original 'Posh and Becks'. Billy and Elaine are so warm, kind and humble and yet, given the enormous success they have both achieved in their respective careers, they could be forgiven for being the opposite. 'Billy, Billy', as he is affectionately known, loved his time at Argyle and maintains it was the best two years of his life, playing alongside the late, great Paul Mariner.

My personal tribute to the great **Paul Mariner:**

I first saw Paul play, would you believe, as a trialist in May 1973 at Penzance. Argyle were on an end-of-season tour in Cornwall and Paul scored twice before being substituted. He scored the following night at Porthlevan and again on the Friday at St Austell. In all three games, he was substituted. When he asked Tony Waiters, then Argyle's manager, why, after coming all this way, he was being constantly taken off, Tony's reply was: 'You are scoring too many goals; with every goal you score your price is going up.' It was evident from the beginning that Paul was a class act, and it was no surprise when he signed from Chorley during that summer at the age of nineteen.

The start of the 73/74 season was not a good one for Argyle and with Paul scoring regularly for Plymouth

Argyle Reserves, he was given his debut at Home Park on Tuesday 11 September 1973 against Rochdale. Alan Rogers and Brian Johnson also made their debuts that night. From the Devonport end, I saw Paul score twice in a 5–0 victory. The rest, as they say, is history. As I have previously mentioned, in those days I used to collect autographs and would be by the Players' Entrance before and after games, so slowly got to talk to Paul. It was only 'the great goal, great performance' type of conversation but we knew each other.

Anyone who witnessed the 74/75 season could not help being blown away by the Mariner/Rafferty partnership.

Argyle were promoted as runners up, with Paul scoring twenty-one goals and winning the player of the season award whilst Billy scored twenty-six goals. A friendship was born between Paul and Billy and remained until the sad day of Paul's passing.

Attendances were soaring and away trips were a joy to behold. 7–3 at Bournemouth, 5–1 at Hereford, 3–3 at Crystal Palace and going 2 up at Blackburn only to lose 5–2. Season 75/76 saw Argyle consolidate in the old Second Division and Paul top scored again with sixteen league and cup goals. He also won player of the season for the second year in a row. It was obvious by now that it was only a matter of time before he moved to a big club. Sure enough, Paul was transferred to Ipswich Town in October 1976; I was devasted.

The 76/77 season was dreadful with Argyle being relegated. Paul returned to Argyle to play in Jim Furnell's testimonial at the end of the season and surprisingly didn't score.

I then lost touch with Paul as his career spiralled into greatness with huge success at Ipswich, England and, to a lesser degree, Arsenal.

In 2004 I became involved with Argyle Legends and when Paul returned as head coach with Argyle in 2009, he had no hesitation in joining the Legends. From then until his passing, Paul kept in touch with me from all over the world and was one of the most humble, loyal and great ambassadors for the club. He used to call Argyle his extended family. He supported us in our game against Liverpool Legends and nothing was ever too much trouble.

Paul's last visit to Plymouth was in February 2019 for the Tony Waiters' reunion. Both Paul and Billy were in fine form that weekend and brought the house down with their double act at the Sunday lunch.

I just wish to conclude by saying: 'Good night, my friend, sleep tight; the world is a lesser place without you.'

RIP – Argyle Legend

Tommy and Elaine Tynan – It would be unforgivable of me not to include Tommy and Elaine Tynan in this category. I often pinch myself to confirm I am not dreaming, and we really have become great friends. Tommy was one of my heroes in the 80s and undoubtedly the main man at Argyle for several seasons. I could never have imagined that I would be spending time talking politics at his home with him and with his lovely wife Elaine. I have also almost become his part-time chauffeur, taking him to several events across the city. A fiercely loyal man, in my humble opinion, and I hope our friendship continues for many years to come. I believe Tommy has a lot more untold stories remaining.

John and Sue Hore – My list of great friends could go on forever. I think I could write a book on these alone. Once again, without wishing to bore the reader, I must mention John and Sue Hore. I have known John for over twenty years, since he was appointed president of the Former Players Association, known then as Argyle Legends. John even had a season or two as the match-day host in the Tribute Lounge at Home Park. I cannot thank him enough for all his help down the years. To me, our secret missions to Exeter City to cheer on Argyle are legendary. Collars up, caps on, real secret service stuff. As for Sue, a lovely, charming lady who makes the best pasties ever.

Steve and Jan Davey – Another couple of whom I can't speak highly enough. Steve is my 'go to' guy, when I struggle to source a match-day guest. I have been privileged to know the whole family over the years and they are all great people. Thank you for letting me into your lives.

Kevin and Carol Hodges – Two more very good friends I can't leave out. Not only is Kevin the record appearance holder for the football club, but I also believe he holds the record for the longest single telephone call: two hours and five minutes. Our telephone conversations are epic. There is always plenty to chat about and we never talk for less than an hour. When the phone rings and Kev's number pops up, I always think: *Well, that's the next hour of my life sorted.* Seriously, I wouldn't change them for the world. Once again, I am so humbled to be doing what I do. And finally, Kev, I insist on buying breakfast next time.

Tony and Anne Waiters – one of the proudest moments during my time running Argyle Legends was organising the Tony Waiters' forty-year reunion weekend on 22, 23 and 24 February 2019.

Tony had not been back to Plymouth since he was dismissed from the Club in April 1977 after being manager for 1,653 days. You cannot imagine how delighted I was when Tony and his beautiful family, wife Anne, daughter Victoria and son-in-law Patrick, accepted my invitation to return after all those years.

The weekend was a tremendous success with sixteen former players joining Tony and his family for three days of celebration. I had never met Tony before but from the moment we said 'Hello' when he arrived after a twenty-seven-hour journey from Vancouver, Canada, we immediately 'hit it off'. There were three major events lined up for him: an evening with Tony and former players on the Friday night, matchday guest for the home game versus Rochdale the following day (which Argyle won 5–1) and the major event, lunch with Tony Waiters at the Duke of Cornwall Hotel, Plymouth, on the Sunday.

This event was a complete sell-out, and the hotel entrance was lined with autograph hunters from all over the country. Considering Tony at this time was eighty-two years old, had travelled for twenty-seven hours to get to Plymouth and was already the guest of honour for the two previous days, his stamina and enthusiasm were outstanding. He never refused a 'selfie' or an autograph and had time for everyone.

Tony told me he wished he could have remained at the football club because he certainly had unfinished business. Anne was also brilliant throughout the weekend and Victoria had never previously been to Plymouth.

Sadly, Tony was to pass away in November 2020, but he became a special friend in such a short space of time. Anne and I remain friends to this day.

Tony Waiters at Home Park flanked by
Billy, Billy (Rafferty) – left –
and the great Paul Mariner – right

Graham and Irene Little – My first meeting with the late, great Graham Little came when we were both invited onto *BBC Spotlight* to talk about our memories of the Santos game. Graham was club secretary at Argyle for over twenty-five years; he talked about his role in staging the Santos match whilst I talked about it from the point of view of an avid fan.

From that day, right up to his passing in November 2021, Graham and I became firm friends. It was my immense pleasure to spend many afternoons at Graham's house discussing our joint love of Argyle. Graham's lovely wife, Irene, would serve up custard creams, cup-cakes and countless cups of tea; we were like kids in a sweet shop.

Graham would recall vividly the people he met during his time at the club and I would keep him up to date on the current activities of those players.

Two of my other standout memories involving Graham are 'An evening with Dave Smith' in June 2018 as well as 'An evening with Graham' himself in October 2018, both of these events were held at Home Park.

Sadly, Graham's health was beginning to deteriorate but my regular visits continued up to a few weeks before his death. I am now the proud owner of some of Graham's memorabilia.

Mike and Ginny Trebilcock – Mike played for Argyle from April 1963 until December 1965, scoring twenty-nine goals before moving to Everton. Mike scored twice for the 'Toffees' (the nickname of Everton Football Club) in the 1966 Wembley Cup Final against Sheffield Wednesday and was a player I had wanted to sign up to Argyle Legends for a very long time, and like Tony Waiters, Mike (who then lived in Australia) had not been back to England for many years.

You can only imagine my surprise when I received a call from Aiden Maher (Aiden played seventy times for Argyle between 1968 and 1970) telling me that Mike was back in England for a short visit and I should expect a telephone call from a number in Liverpool. A couple of days later my mobile rang and it was Mike. Aiden had told him all about Argyle Legends and Mike was keen to be involved. The call could not have gone better and at the end of it I felt as if I had known Mike for a lifetime. He gave me his various contact details and I thought: *Job done*. About a week later, my phone rang again; it was Mike asking me if he could come to a game: 'Of course,' I replied, and on Sunday

15 May 2016, Mike was the match-day guest at the Play-Off semi-final against Portsmouth. I was able to reunite Mike with John Hore and Aiden Maher. *Mike is a really nice fella*, I thought. *It's a shame he is going back to Australia.* I was mistaken. A couple of weeks later, Mike phoned me to say: 'I haven't gone back; I'm getting married to Ginny.' Who is Ginny, I hear you say? Ginny was Mike's childhood sweetheart, and fifty-two years after Mike left Plymouth for Everton, they finally got married on Friday 30 September 2016, and guess what – I was honoured to be invited to their wedding.

Mike was becoming somewhat of a regular at Home Park and attended the Newport game on Monday 17 April 2017 when Argyle won 6–1, gaining promotion from Division Two.

On Saturday 22 December 2018 I was able to reunite Mike with Norman Piper, Steve Davey and Dave Lean at the home game against Accrington Stanley. It was a great day despite Argyle losing 3–0.

Chris and Angie Harrison, John and Nicola Uzzell, Leigh and Karen Cooper, Ronnie Mauge, Chris Hargreaves and David Norris are all people I have become close to and class as good friends. I constantly have to pinch myself to believe it's true.

Random Memories

The following is a series of random memories by Phil, Paul's brother, who accompanied Paul and Norman on some of the away trips as a younger companion!

Monday 26 August 1968

Away to Exeter City in a second-round replay in the first round of the League Cup.

In those days, there were replays and second replays on a neutral ground if the scores were still level after the first two games. Argyle's replay was at Plainmoor, the home ground of Torquay United.

Although the game was extremely tense, with the winning goal not coming for Exeter City until the 119th minute, an event in itself which was very disturbing because Argyle were expected to win against the team from a lower division, the most disturbing event for me was my first direct experience of physical aggression at a football game.

After the game, a large group of Plymouth fans made their way from the ground to where the coaches were parked and some were chanting: 'We are a right load of bastxxxx when we lose.' Suddenly, and without warning, a bottle was thrown through the window of one of the houses that was very close to the Plymouth fans.

I continued as part of the away fans to move towards where the coaches were parked but always being hungry, I could not resist going to a nearby fish and chip shop to get some food. On entering the shop, I came upon a scene where three middle-aged men, who were not pleased at all about having a bottle thrown through the window of their house, were trying to provoke some of the Plymouth fans in the shop to step outside. None of the Plymouth fans obliged, but I do remember one of them applying logic to the situation by asking: 'How do you know it was one of us?' The response duly given by the main aggressor was: 'Because you are wearing these fxxxing colours.' He had flipped the tassels of the Plymouth Argyle Rosette that was worn by the fan who had dared to apply logic to the situation.

Although not being the bravest of youths, I did stay to buy my food and then returned to Paul and Norman and narrated my story. I guess the full impact of the episode could not make a large impression on them because they had not witnessed the incident, but I do remember feeling a little less secure on away trips following that night's experience.

Saturday 26 October 1968

Argyle were playing a league match away to Gillingham, Kent. From what I remember, there were many fans who left Plymouth Station on the 'football special' bound for Paddington. Paul, Norman and I were with a group of friends and the journey from Plymouth to London seemed to pass quite quickly. I remember one guy who lost what seemed at the time to be quite a bit of money in a card game. When we arrived in London, we had to make the next stage of the journey by taking a train to Gillingham. In those days, the total journey from Plymouth to Gillingham was about five hours, not including time spent in transferring from train to train.

When we arrived at Gillingham station, the transport police ordered us to line up because they wanted to search us. It took quite a long time for this search process to be carried out and one of our friends, who always considered himself to be quite comical and courageous, asked one of the police officers if they thought he had a machine gun under his hat. Not wishing to lose face to our friend, the police officer violently snatched the hat from his head and assured him that another such question would mean he would be watching the four walls of a very small room as opposed to a football match. We later heard that a green flag belonging to the guard of the train had been stolen during the journey and that, because of this search, it had been retrieved. As an aside, it's interesting to note that in those days, trains employed a guard as part of their staff.

When we entered the ground, we were escorted to the away end where there was no crowd segregation; and very soon, fireworks were being thrown at us because some of the home fans had purchased them in advance of Bonfire Night on Tuesday 5 November. I'm aware that I mentioned a 'Guy' on the train to London, but I hadn't anticipated that there would be a connection between him and the fireworks!

As the fireworks were flying, and because in those days fans could freely walk from one part of the ground to the other, we went to the other end of the ground to support the Greens. Shortly into the second half, Gillingham took the lead (going on to win 1–0) and we were feeling pretty despondent. But not as despondent as when groups of hostile home fans began to make the move from other parts of the ground towards us. Not very reassuringly, a policeman advised us to look out for a particular person who had recently been released from prison and who was known to be violent. I appreciate the policeman was trying to give us advanced warning, but his words had certainly unsettled us because one of our party, called George Taylor, half comically and half seriously said that he didn't fancy seeing his dinner a second time around (I believe he was referring to the fact that a bladed article might reveal the contents of his stomach).

None of us wanted to stay to see if the home fans were going to give us a warm reception (the Bonfire Night image goes on), and so we decided to leave the ground early. There was no obvious exit from the ground (perhaps in our panic we had not noticed one), and so we proceeded to climb a very high gate to escape from the ground and made our way directly to the station for an early return to London. Once again, within the space of two months, I had directly witnessed aggression at a football game and the Gillingham incident seemed to be more serious than the one in Torquay in August earlier that year.

Saturday 15 February 1969

Argyle were playing away at Orient (as that football team were then known, before reverting to their previous name of Leyton Orient in 1987) and so a trip to London was involved. This trip would prove to be very memorable for me as I shall later describe. The game was very exciting, and we won 2–1 with a goal in the first and second halves. The first one was scored by Richard Reynolds after only one minute and forty seconds (that is what I recall, but I am prepared to be challenged on this fact). We spent the evening in London because, as usual, the 'football special' train left Paddington at midnight.

There was a lot of rain in London that evening as we were walking around the sights of Soho. Through the eyes of a –fifteen-year-old boy, the sights and lights appeared even more spectacular than perhaps they probably were. One of our group, called Roger Wakeham, decided that we should watch a striptease show in the El Paradise Club in Brewer Street in order to escape from the rain! He negotiated an entrance fee and we were quickly ushered into the building. The narrow corridor from the entrance to the striptease stage was very dimly lit and afterwards, Roger confessed that, at first, he thought we were going to be mugged. However, we were shown to our seats in the front row and the show began. Even now, I still recall how shy and embarrassed I was, and the performers quickly identified this weakness in me and made more of a show for me than they would perhaps have done for another person.

I really was dreadfully embarrassed when one of the performers, taking Norman's scarf from his neck, proceeded to warm parts of her body that perhaps a scarf is not associated with. I remember we stayed in the El Paradise Club for about an hour before leaving. I do recall a lot of our friends were very amused at my reaction to the show and I think probably had a laugh at my expense.

126

Having to sleep on the floor of the mail carriage on the way home was no hardship and I was relieved to be back in Plymouth early on the Sunday morning.

However, I was clearly not shocked enough to have left behind the programme that was part of the entrance fee and wanted to keep it as a souvenir. I decided to hide it in my mother's piano, thinking that it was safe and sound, never to be found. How wrong can you be! My mother, some months later, decided to spring clean her piano and produced the programme for me to provide an explanation. I was very surprised that she seemed unfazed by the matter, probably seeing it as just part of my growing up. Had she realised how embarrassed I had been, she would probably have laughed as well.

I'm not sure now why I was so embarrassed, but perhaps it was because Paul and I had no sisters, and I went to a single-sex school. Once again, how times have changed! Single-sex schools are very rare nowadays and our society is more open to discussing relationships.

Saturday 1 March 1969

Argyle were playing away to Crewe Alexandra (Cheshire) in a league match, and we travelled on a supporters' coach which left Bretonside Coach Station, Plymouth, at midnight on the Friday before the game, arriving in Crewe at about seven in the morning. We had to wait until cafes opened to get breakfast, and so we played football in a park to pass the time. One of our friends had brought a plastic football with them (as you do)!

I must say that I had never seen so much dog excrement in such abundance in such a concentrated area, and the expression 'tread carefully' took on a new meaning. We eventually managed to get breakfast and spent the rest of the morning and early afternoon exploring Crewe! We made our way to the ground and took our places in the wooden stand of a very old and underdeveloped ground. Plymouth were on a very good unbeaten run, as I remember, and our opponents were not having a good season and so we expected to win. We put a lot of early pressure on the home team and, after missing many good chances, we took the lead in the seventeenth minute with a penalty. Sadly, by half time the home team had equalised and went on to score the winner in the second half.

Having expected to win quite comfortably, we were very disconsolate to have lost. But our disappointment quickly turned to fear because outside the ground, many groups of home fans were surrounding and beating up any Argyle fans they came across. The situation was scary for what seemed to be a long time and we walked faster and faster back towards the centre of the town. Fortunately, one of our quick-thinking friends flagged down a taxi and we all jumped in. Whether or not it was because the driver was female and, therefore, a little more sympathetic than perhaps a male driver would have been, I really don't know, but she did not hesitate to take six of us in a four-passenger taxi. I distinctly remember lying across the laps of four of my friends who were squashed into the back seats. Strangely, we then had tea in a relatively quiet cafe and waited until it was time to go to the coaches to take us home.

So it was becoming an unexpected theme that physical aggression and violence appeared to be quite normal and accepted in the late 1960s. I have often read about the phenomenon of football fans' physical aggression and violence, but it was not until I began to contribute to Paul and Norman's story that I realised how much it had been a part of my lived experience.

Saturday 3 October 1970

The fifth and final episode in the series of my recollections of my football adventures with Paul and Norman features Argyle playing away to Fulham at Craven Cottage on the banks of the River Thames, London, which ended in a one-all draw. After the game, because the 'football special' train left Paddington at the usual time of midnight, we spent the evening at the home of Norman's mother as opposed to walking around the streets of London.

I knew that Norman's parents had separated and that his mother had gone to live in London with his siblings. What seems a very strange thing to be writing is that I was surprised to learn that the inside of a London home was very similar to that of a Plymouth one. In my naivety, having never visited a London home before, I guess I was expecting it to be completely different from the homes I was used to in Plymouth. It's strange now to think of how I imagined the world to be at the age of fifteen.

Elsewhere in this book, Paul and Norman mention my mother, whom Norman used to affectionately refer to as Mrs H. I am pleased to say that I look upon Norman as a brother and, indeed, many friends of my mother often said that he was the fourth son in her family. I also firmly believe that had the opportunity presented itself, my mother would have legally adopted Norman. I'm simply referring to this now because thinking of the time when I visited the home of Norman's mother has brought back to me the fact that after his mother moved to London, and Norman stayed in Plymouth, he increasingly became part of Paul's life and mine and, hence, he became more like a brother than a friend.

I must say that I did not appreciate how my becoming involved in this account of Norman and Paul's story would prove to be cathartic and therapeutic. However, before I become too philosophical and emotional, let's return to the golden thread of football, which runs through Paul and Norman's book and, hence, through my five episodes.

During the evening at Norman's mother's house, I watched *Match of the Day* and witnessed, as did thousands of other fans, the 'Goal of the Season' scored against Everton by Ernie Hunt of Coventry City, after an outrageous freekick manoeuvre by his teammate, Willie Carr. This trick, known as the 'Donkey Kick', was immediately banned by the FA, but it was a fabulous sight to behold and the Everton goalkeeper, Andy Rankin, was left as utterly amazed and bemused by this incident as the rest of us were.

I am very privileged to be able to make a short, direct contribution to Paul and Norman's book and I feel that I realise now, more than ever, how much football is about friendships, memories and a sense of belonging. Paul and Norman, my brothers, I do hope that others appreciate and value your account as much as I do.

Ode to 'Green Harts Forever'

This book was not too hard to write;
As our shared experiences came in sight.
We, Paul and Norm, had many a smile;
Writing about the Greens of Plymouth Argyle.

We hope so much you've enjoyed this book;
And will encourage others to take a look.
We've followed Argyle from boy to man;
And strike a chord with you, we're sure we can.

For both us men our team means so much;
Its friendship and unity we daily touch.
Supporting them is never a chore;
The Greens from Plymouth that we 'Janners' adore.

Our Friendship is still cooking on Gas!

Milton Keynes UK
Ingram Content Group UK Ltd.
UKHW022242101124
450923UK00005B/7